THE BEST OF
REMINISCE.

CONTENTS

REMINISCE

ASSOCIATE CREATIVE DIRECTOR
Christina Spalatin
EXECUTIVE EDITOR Kirsten Schrader
DEPUTY EDITOR Mary-Liz Shaw
ART DIRECTOR Kristen Stecklein
ASSOCIATE EDITOR Julie Kuczynski
COPY EDITOR Amy Rabideau Silvers
PRODUCTION COORDINATOR
Jon Syverson
SENIOR RIGHTS ASSOCIATE Jill Godsey

PICTURED ON FRONT COVER
Wedded couple on page 50,
    Robert J. Murray
Serviceman on page 119, Roger Hill
Young couple on page 69,
    Norma Wingert
Kids in red coats on page 23,
    Susan Lyons Dietrich
Dancing girl on page 24, Linda Knox
Family in sunglasses on page 87,
    Tamara Moran-Smith

PICTURED ON BACK COVER
Siblings on page 29, H. Clark Dean

ADDITIONAL PHOTO CREDIT
Vintage scrapbook page,
OHishiapply/Shutterstock

© 2020 RDA Enthusiast Brands, LLC.
1610 N. 2nd St., Suite 102
Milwaukee, WI 53212-3906

International Standard Book Number:
D 978-1-61765-908-9
U 978-1-61765-909-6
Component Number:
D 117300066H
U 117300068H
International Standard Serial Number:
2689-1786

TAKING THE FIFTH

Our class of 4-year-olds at the Phyllis Ann Dance Studio in Bellingham posed in ballet's fifth position in 1941. I'm in the center. All these years later I'm still in touch with friends from those wonderful days.

KAREN BOWSHER KOHLWES · CLINTON, WA

Some connections to the past we never lose—like the friendship shared among the beaming, pint-size ballerinas at left. We hope this new keepsake collection of stories and photos from the previous year of *Reminisce* will have you looking back at the connections in your own life that have stood the test of time.

The Best of Reminisce has cherished memories of growing up, especially tender moments spent with family. You'll find stories of true love, including one of a couple who met in grade school, and read how some could find fun in unexpected places, such as home ec class. We have a compelling account about women who kept up the homefront when men left in wartime, and personal reflections from those who served and longed to be back home.

And, of course, there are those colorful spots of pop culture that are always a delight to revisit: cars with gigantic fins, decked-out campers, surprising celebrity encounters and vintage ads that are eye-popping—and occasionally hilarious.

We're glad you've joined us on this journey into the best of the past. Enjoy.

THE EDITORS OF *REMINISCE* MAGAZINE

CHAPTER 1

GROWING UP

Take a step back in time to the carefree days of youth, when life ran at a different pace for tykes and teens alike.

Pedal Power

In 1955, the boys and I rode our tractors and bicycles up
and down the sidewalk on our block in Montpelier, Ohio.
From left are Tommy, Jerry, Ronnie, me and my brother, Doug.
The tractor I'm on was Doug's. I traded him for my tricycle.
When playing outside, we often wore T-shirts and bib overalls.

ELLYN COCHRAN SCARLETT · ELKHART, IN

Dede gets ready to take to the streets of Chichester, New Hampshire.

Put Her in Drive

The time had come to take the wheel.

———

Learning to drive was never really something I thought about. When my brother Lew and I entered our freshman year of high school in Concord, New Hampshire, our sister Polly, who was a senior, drove us the 10 miles every day from our home in Chichester. After Polly graduated, Lew took over the driving. But once Lew and I graduated, my parents realized that I'd managed to skip an important rite of passage—and they were shocked that I didn't care to learn.

"When you get married, you can't depend on your husband to do all the driving," Mom told me. "You can't expect your neighbors to do it either."

So my journey to the world of driving began in 1956 with my folks giving me a gray 1949 Plymouth with standard transmission. Dad showed me how to start it and shift gears, but the rest was up to me. We lived way out in the country opposite a narrow dirt road that ran through woods. About 2 miles in, there was a slight hill. Dad's rule was I had to stop on the crest of the hill and hold the car steady by jockeying the clutch and the gas, without stalling, for several minutes before I could drive on.

It was important to get the trick down because there was a stoplight at the top of a large hill at a key intersection in downtown Concord. If I stalled at that light, I'd hold up most of the city traffic.

Top: The Marston family fleet includes three Chevys, a Jeep and a Ford pickup. Above: Unlike his sister, Lew was a born driver.

GIVE IT A BRAKE

As soon as I passed my driver's test in 1958, the power of my newfound independence surging through me, I got behind the wheel, admired myself in the rearview mirror, shifted into reverse—and backed our family's brand-new car right into a utility pole.

CHARLENE BUNAS
SANTA ROSA, CA

POWER STEERING

In mid-1953, I scheduled a road test for my Illinois driver's license, but before I could take it, the state decided to raise the legal driving age to 16, which meant I would have to wait a whole year before I could reschedule—an outrage! I wrote an impassioned letter to the secretary of state demanding that I be allowed to take my test *immediately.* To my shock, he agreed. So through sheer chutzpah I was one of the last people in Illinois to get a license at 15.

ALAN BONE
WEST NEWTON, MA

No one ever went with me on my jaunts through the woods, except for my dog, Lady. She refused to stay behind, but as soon as we got home, she'd scramble out of the car and shake uncontrollably. Lew theorized the poor thing was terrified of my driving. Perhaps my battles with the clutch at the little hill were too much for her.

Mr. Bartlett at the motor vehicle department was a family friend. When it was time for my road test, instead of taking me around the usual busy route in Concord, Mr. Bartlett had me drive the deserted half-mile stretch from his house in tiny Epsom, New Hampshire, to the Methodist church and back. Naturally, I passed with flying colors. "She won't have any problems," he told my father.

It's a good thing neither of them could see into the future. Between getting lost countless times and going the wrong way on one-way streets, I was probably responsible for all the women-driver jokes. A few years later someone rear-ended my gray Plymouth, but not before I customized a fence during a snowstorm.

It wasn't until I moved to Florida in 1985 that I took a real driver's test. The first thing the instructor had me do was take my car to a mechanic to get the horn fixed. I hadn't even known it was broken—I'd never used it.

DEDE MARSTON HAMMOND
ZEPHYRHILLS, FL

Her first passport in hand in 1952, Barbara was all set to face her future.

Flying Solo

That new ID was a passport to independence.

G rowing up in a military family, I had seen quite a bit of the world before my teen years, but traveling with my mother and on her passport.

Shortly after my 12th birthday in 1952, my parents made a startling announcement: My mother would be renewing her passport and I would not be included on it. I had to get my own because I was going away to school in Switzerland.

This was well before the European Union, so passports had to be presented at every border throughout the continent. In my case, I would have to travel back and forth to Switzerland by myself several times a year. My parents knew, too, that I soon would have opportunities to travel with school groups and friends.

You weren't allowed to smile for passport photos, but I was so pleased and excited about

getting my own identification that I found it difficult to keep a straight face for the camera. Somehow I managed it. That summer my mother and I were back in the United States, and on our return to Europe I proudly carried my very own passport.

After flying into Frankfort, Germany, we took an overnight train to Paris, France. Imagine my surprise at being awakened in the middle of the night with the adults to sign my entry papers at the French border—something Mother previously had been able to do for me.

I enjoyed so many adventures on that and subsequent passports. Fortunately, I married a man who loves to travel as much as I do, so I have not been without an active passport to this day.

BARBARA SETHMANN · TAPPAHANNOCK, VA

EVERYONE PITCHED IN

DURING WORLD WAR II, MY SCHOOL CHUMS AND

I went to Raymond Avenue Elementary School in Los Angeles, California. The entire school participated in the war effort with a push to buy war savings stamps. Stamps cost as little as 10 cents, and every $18.75 collected could be converted to a $25 savings bond.

A drawing of a military ambulance hung on the cafeteria wall, and a portion of it was colored in every time one of us purchased a stamp. When we achieved our goal, the Army sent a jeep and a soldier to drive us around the school grounds. Now, that was exciting!

By 1945, the war was over and we were at Horace Mann Junior High. It was a wonderful time to grow up.

FRED CASSTEVENS · TORRANCE, CA

Six friends were in junior high in 1945. In the back row, from left, are Frank Fitzpatrick, Durward "Bud" Falkenstein and Fred. Standing in front are Bill Gallagher and Ted Amlick, and seated is Bob Boydston.

STREET LEGAL

Forty years ago, the only rite of passage that mattered to me was obtaining a coveted New York State sheriff's ID card, the 18-year-old's license to drink legally in the late '60s and '70s. And wouldn't you know it, not one bar bouncer asked for it that first summer after I got mine.
MIKE McCROBIE · OSWEGO, NY

At 18, Phyllis cast her vote for George McGovern.

PRIDE IN A CIVIL RIGHT

Brooklyn's Avenue M bustled with its usual energy on that first Tuesday in November 1972. The train station was the focal point of the street—and it was our family meeting place at 5 p.m.

"Today is your big day," Dad said to me with a smile. He was as proud as I was that I would be voting in the presidential election for the first time.

My parents and I walked to East 19th Street and joined the line of people waiting to vote. As I closed the curtain on the booth, I was overwhelmed by the moment. I had arrived!

I voted for George McGovern that year, and even though he lost, I still remember well the exhilaration of pulling the lever to have my opinion counted.

I hope young people get out and take a stand on issues that are important to them. It does matter. It does affect you.
PHYLLIS WEINBERGER
NORTH WOODMERE, NY

Al Was a Straight Shooter

He didn't play ball, but he was a pro at the game of life.

Summers during high school in the early 1960s, I worked on a beef farm for Al Spanier, a 47-year-old bachelor. He was kind—a man who always wore a smile. I did field work, fed the cattle and cut the lawn with a push mower for $50 a month. He'd bring me my pay from what he called "a safe place," which was somewhere behind the machine shed.

One day I asked Al if I could put up a basketball hoop at the shed, which had a cement slab in front of it. The next day, while I was cultivating corn in the north forty, Al went to town on a few errands. That night I found a hoop on the shed door above the slab. When I went in for supper, there in my chair was a brand-new Spaulding basketball. It was Christmas in July.

I'd spend my evenings shooting buckets. After a couple of weeks, Al decided he wanted to try. I showed him how to shoot—"It's all in the wrists," I told him—but Al just wasn't coordinated enough to get the ball up over the rim. So he lowered the basket.

Senior year, after my third and last summer at Al's farm, we had a basketball game against our rival, the Albany Huskies. Despite a snowstorm that day, we had a packed house. It was close through the third quarter when I was fouled. The crowd went quiet as I stepped up to the free-throw line. I missed the first one, but then I heard someone in the stands.

"It's all in the wrists!"

It was Al, who was at his first-ever high school basketball game.

We ended up losing the game, but Al came up to me later and shook my hand. "Some of those guys can jump really high," he said.

I didn't see Al very often after that. I went to college for a while, then joined the Navy. Eventually I met a woman and we made wedding plans. I wanted to invite Al, so I went out to his farm, where I saw that the hoop was still hanging a non-regulation 8 feet up on the door of the shed.

Al came to my wedding with his bride, a widow he'd always been sweet on who owned a bar in town. For a gift he gave me a 10-gallon milk can, telling me to put money in it every payday and keep it in a safe place.

At Al's funeral in 1996, one of his relatives told me, "Al never trusted banks. He kept all of his money in a milk can buried in the ground behind his machine shed." So it hadn't been an emergency fund back there; it was his entire savings.

I feel very fortunate to have had Al in my life while I was growing up. He'll always have a safe place in my heart.

Dale learned how to be a good person from a farmer named Al.

DALE HENNEN
PAYNESVILLE, MN

Jeri holds her doll and purse next to Mom, Gusty, while sister Caroline shields her eyes from the sun in this picture taken in the Hagginwood neighborhood of Sacramento in 1942.

Mom Doled Out Sage Advice

Watching the kids digging in the dirt may have had something to do with it.

As a child born in 1936, I remember often hearing my mother say, "Don't forget to wash behind your ears." Mothers don't say that anymore, and I may have figured out why.

In those days, children only bathed about once a week, and it was usually on Saturday night. So of course they were ready for a good soak in the tub.

As I thought more about it, another contributing factor came to mind: There were no video games, TV or computers back then. And guess what? We all played outside.

I remember the fort that my sister and I, along with several neighborhood kids, spent many hours making. We dug tunnels about 3 feet deep in a vacant field next door to our house and covered them with boards and more dirt. We left a couple of access doors so we could get in and out, and also have some light. And we played king of the mountain on the excavated dirt pile.

Yes, today an activity of this kind would probably be considered a dangerous pastime, but we weren't so accident-conscious then.

We spent many hours in our fort, laughing, giggling and pretending. Mom had only to look out the kitchen window to keep an eye on us.

Looking back, I remember sitting in the bathtub and being surprised at how much dirt was behind my ears. Even more surprising was the big dirt ring around the tub after the water was drained.

JERI MULLER · NEWCASTLE, CA

Kathy rode her stick horse, Buttermilk, similar to the one at far left, up and down the trails.

Git Along Little Dogies

Mounting that wooden pony
launched many adventurous rides.

My heroes have always been cowboys, just like in the Willie Nelson song. I fell in love with Roy Rogers in 1953, dressed like Dale Evans, and nearly wore down my own Buttermilk (named after Dale's horse) to a nub while riding the open ranges of Northern California.

Buttermilk was no beauty. Dad carved her from a piece of oak left over from our new dining room table. He painted her white, cut two leather ears and tacked on a leather bridle. He colored a black mane down her neck and drew gentle eyes on both sides of her head. Her red plastic saddle softened the long trail rides across my aunt's sheep ranch in Albion. Dragging Buttermilk, I herded the sheep, chased squirrels through the woods beyond the pasture and put her to bed in the old red barn at night.

Every Saturday afternoon my older sister, Marie, escorted me to the 25-cent Western matinee. We munched on 10-cent bags of popcorn and watched Roy, Dale, Hopalong Cassidy and Gene Autry ride across the hills and plains on their horses Trigger, Buttermilk, Topper and Champion. After the movies, I hopped on my winsome pony and chased bank robbers through red rock canyons and drove dastardly cattle rustlers across the sagebrush.

On a recent trip to the grocery store, I saw a bin of modern stick horses. Glassy black eyes stared at me from fuzzy brown heads. On an impulse, I squeezed a felt ear. The horse whinnied and a galloping sounded through the store. Sheepishly, I ducked down an aisle. Technology certainly has come a long way since my Buttermilk-riding days.

KATHY MARCELLIN SMITH · ST. LOUIS, MO

THE SWEET SPOT

Candy ads make their mark in a riot of color.

1955 »

Out of This World

This clever ad alludes to portable record players and rock 'n' roll in the mid-1950s. Named for a popular malt shake of the 1920s, Milky Way is the "best-liked chocolate-covered" bar in the world, the ad says. It was known as a Mars bar outside the U.S.

1950 ⌃

One Tough Nut

Founded by an immigrant whose family had escaped the Armenian genocide in Turkey, the Peter Paul Manufacturing Co. started as a small shop in Connecticut. In a tight market, it grew by setting itself apart with products made from exotic ingredients. This ad for Almond Joy, in lush blues and greens, evokes the warmth of the tropics, where the company sourced its coconut.

« 1949

Bold and Beautiful

The candy industry at midcentury was dominated by makers in and around Chicago, Illinois, with Curtiss Candy Co. being one of the largest. It employed more than 2,000 by the mid-1930s. Founder Otto Schnering had a genius for marketing and would do stunts like dropping Baby Ruths from an airplane. This ad from *Life* magazine reflects a go-for-broke style.

Nell had fun with the gang (she's seated on right) and as a cheerleader (center).

Ticket to Adventure

An energetic tomboy puts her two wheels to good use.

Bowling Green, Kentucky, where I was born in the summer of 1929, was a little town where you could leave the windows up and the doors open. There were at least 30 children on my street, making the neighborhood a wonderful playground. I was a tomboy who loved to skate, climb trees and be one of the gang. Hide-and-seek, kick-the-can and building clubhouses out of loose rocks and gathered materials were great fun.

Back then, poodle skirts, saddle Oxfords and crinoline petticoats were all the rage, but my heart was set on earning enough for a bicycle. With World War II underway, new bikes were scarce and costly. Babysitting for 25 cents an hour was a slow route to savings. I'll never forget the birthday when my dear mother added $8 to the $17 I'd collected in my piggy bank, enough to buy a sturdy used bike. Its red paint was dull, but you'd think I'd paid a fortune for this two-wheeler, considering how often I washed and waxed it.

Because my family didn't own a car, that bike took me to the park, the drugstore for milkshakes and any other place I wanted to go.

One special place was a large open area near our house where the neighborhood children loved to play. Blackberries, frogs and water moss made it an interesting hideaway for the gang. This field became even more fascinating when the Army soldiers held training camp under the trees close to the little pond.

The soldiers would often ask me to ride to Elm Grove Dairy to buy lemon custard ice cream for them. As a youngster, that lemon custard ice cream seemed the perfect reward for those hardworking fighting men.

How did I ever manage to get back to the camp without the ice cream melting? Hard work: Because with every push of the pedals, I was helping the war effort and my country.

NELL JOHNSON · BLYTHEVILLE, AR

A TOOTHSOME TALE

A WEEK BEFORE MY 8TH BIRTHDAY IN 1965, my brother Larry brought home a gray velvet box. He set it on the buffet and told me not to touch it. Of course, that only made me want to know what was in it.

I kept pestering him to tell me until, finally, to get me to leave him alone, he admitted that it was my birthday present. But I wasn't to get too excited about it, he said, because it was just a fancy toothbrush. Brushing my teeth wasn't my favorite thing to do, so I quickly lost interest.

When I opened the present on my birthday, instead of the dreaded toothbrush, I saw a beautiful silver bracelet with a single charm engraved with my birthdate. I felt quite grown up and special.

Fifty-three years later, I still wear my charm bracelet, which looks just as pretty as it did the day a wonderful big brother gave it to his pesky little sister.

SUSAN LARKIN CRAIG · CLAREMORE, OK

Larry Larkin bought his little sister, Susan, a grown-up gift for her 8th birthday.

Karen's bracelet, top, notes her accomplishments, including a journalism award; Nancy's, below, features an arrowhead and a church.

CHARMING CONNECTION

FEELING SHAKEN AND FORLORN, I MUST HAVE LOOKED lonesome sitting on the bleachers in gym class. My new school was so big and I saw no one I knew. Then a girl at the far end of the bench called to me.

"Come sit with us," she said.

That's how I met Karen. We were best friends all through junior and senior high school and into college. We stood up at each other's wedding.

In high school we each bought a charm bracelet and filled them with charms that represented special moments in our lives—boyfriends' names, school pennants, awards. Karen added two child charms when she became a mother. We remained friends the rest of our lives, until 2004, when she died of cancer.

A few weeks after her funeral, I received a package from her husband, with the note, "Karen wanted you to have this."

Each time I look at Karen's bracelet, I smile at the wonderful memories she left me, especially those magic words, "Come sit with us."

NANCY MIESSE · LAKE PLACID, FL

In a melting pot of students, Bethel sits in the front row, left, and friend Helen, behind her, is turned in profile.

Friendship Has No Bounds

A presidential executive order uprooted Japanese immigrants and their children.

Darkness cast its shadow on our nation's history when Japanese internment camps were established during World War II. I know. I was in fifth grade when two girls and a boy from my class disappeared.

Before the war, my father, in search of work, moved us from Wyoming to Nebraska and back to Cheyenne. I entered fourth grade during the 1940-'41 school year at Corlett School. There I met a Japanese girl, Helen, and we became good friends.

Sometime in the middle of the following school year, Helen didn't return. It wasn't until I was in high school that I realized what had happened.

After Japan bombed Pearl Harbor on Dec. 7, 1941, many Americans feared that Japanese American citizens would be loyal to the emperor of Japan. They were rounded up and placed in camps surrounded by barbed wire and Army guards. One of those camps was located at Heart Mountain in Wyoming.

Nearly 11,000 Japanese Americans were confined there, making it the state's third-largest town at the time. They were as American as I was, but they lost everything and were made to feel ashamed of their heritage.

Today the Heart Mountain Relocation Camp is on the National Register of Historic Places. The inscription on one of the site's nine markers reads: "May the injustices of the removal and incarceration of 120,000 persons of Japanese ancestry during World War II, two-thirds of whom were American citizens, never be repeated."

BETHEL HENSON · CASTLE ROCK, WA

TROOP 75 GETS ITS FIRST EAGLE SCOUT

WHEN IT CAME TIME TO JOIN THE BOY
Scouts in 1959, I chose Troop 75, sponsored by Newton School in Detroit, Michigan. At my very first meeting, Scoutmaster and Detroit firefighter Layton Day told us that the troop had never had an Eagle Scout. And before he retired as scoutmaster, he wanted to pin the Eagle medal on a Scout.

That stuck with me, and off I went through the first ranks of Scouting. I took hikes and learned about first aid, map reading, nature, swimming, camping and cooking. We even learned Morse code and other ways to send signals.

Then came the 21 merit badges necessary to earn the Eagle award. A new adventure or field of learning opened up with each badge.

I made new friends through Scouting, and I'm still close with several of them. Three years after

I joined Troop 75, Scoutmaster Day was proud to pin Troop 75's first Eagle award onto my shirt.

Now, 60 years later, I serve as the historian for Kansas City's Scout Council and return to camp each year to assist today's youth on their trail to becoming Eagle Scouts.

ANDY DUBILL · OVERLAND PARK, KS

ALWAYS PREPARED
Fellow Scouts at Camp Giesburg on Bean Lake, Missouri, in 1920 elected members of the Square Deal Party, from left, Walter Wingett, mayor, Clarence Abbott, athletic commissioner, and Charles McBratney, food commissioner, to run day-to-day operations.

Dancing Around the Problem

Her ballet dreams delayed, she leapt at a new career.

When I was a little girl, I loved to dance—what little girl doesn't? If you pinched me hard enough, I bet I could still perform "The Mama Doll Song" that my cousin and I did for every Masonic lodge and Lions Club in town in 1955.

But something terrible happened to me when I was 7. I became sick very suddenly and no one could figure out what was wrong. I was confined to bed for almost a year—I remember the worst part was being too ill to enjoy Christmas. I was carried out to the front room to sit near the tree with my presents, but I was too tired to open them and begged to be taken back to bed. Looking over my mom's shoulder as we left the room, I saw my big brother in tears. It was then that I realized they all thought I was going to die.

We never did find out what had happened to me, but much later I was diagnosed with lupus; I've had many more attacks to fight off in my life.

The doctor told my parents that I'd never be strong enough to take dancing again, which broke my heart. For years, I could only watch as other girls went to their ballet, tap and jazz lessons.

Finally, at 16, I couldn't stand it any longer. I told my mother I was going back to dance school and nothing was going to stop me. Mom reluctantly agreed, saying that I could try one class during the summer session "and we'll see how you do."

Well, I did great! My teacher said I was a natural, but I'd resumed dancing too late in life. There was no way to make up for the years of training I'd missed while my body was growing.

"I can't make you into a dancer," she told me. "But I can train you to be a teacher."

Ye gods and little fishes! Did she just throw me a lifeline, or what?

For the next several years I trained with her, learning all the basic ballet I'd missed, plus the other dance forms I'd need to know. In college, I majored in performing arts and got my master's in drama/dance.

Almost immediately, I was offered a job at Shasta College in Redding, where I'd been a teaching assistant in dance. So I had a job I loved for many years, until I met my husband and we moved out of the area for his work.

Most of my students were adults, and many of them had longed to take dancing lessons when they were children, but their parents hadn't been able to afford them. They all vowed never to perform on stage, but come spring, they would be kicking for joy to the music at our recital.

Listening to the audience, I loved hearing the delighted cries of "That's my mom!" from their own grown children and the shouts of "Go, Granny, go!" from their proud grandchildren.

Danni was an aspiring ballerina in 1952 before illness forced her to hang up her slippers for several years.

DANNI BAYLES-YEAGER
SAN BERNARDINO, CA

Greta tapped like a pro in the well-tailored outfits her mother sewed on an old treadle machine.

You Gotta Have a Gimmick

First rule of showbiz: Always look fabulous!

My introduction to the performing arts came in 1938 when I was almost 6, and Mother signed me up for dance lessons with Miss Spanner, a pretty lady with ruby red lips and dark wavy hair.

Mother and I walked to the dance studio in the west end of Bridgeport, Connecticut, where I'd sit as she tied my shoes. I loved being looked after so caringly by my mother on those Saturdays; during the week she worked at a factory.

There were about 10 of us in the class. At recital time, we had to learn two songs, "The Band Played On" and "She's Only a Bird in a Gilded Cage."

Mother was very crafty and made both of my outfits. I found the band costume uncomfortable, but it was colorful—a chartreuse jacket and spats, both of felt, with a skirt of red and white stripes.

I had the part of the bird in the cage, and the act opened with me on a swing in my costume of white satin chintz patterned in Kelly green polka-dots.

The skirt puffed out, thanks to layers of crinoline, and the hat, cut from cardboard, was covered in the same fabric as the dress. I felt special in that costume and tapped my little heart out.

GRETA DAWSON · BLAIRSVILLE, GA

TO BE A KID AGAIN

SUMMER LIVING

Here are all the Badey cousins celebrating summer vacation at a cottage on Reeds Beach, New Jersey. This picture represents one of my happiest childhood memories. I'm the one with the curly blond hair at the back.

PATRICIA MOORE
TASLEY, VA

PUT UP YOUR DUKES

Wearing boxing gloves, my sister Barbara Zajdel Tennutti, right, and I pose in 1955 for our uncle, who was a photographer. I was 6 at the time and got the shiner a few days earlier by walking into a doorknob at my Chicago, Illinois, home.

CELINE ZAJDEL KILBURG
SARASOTA, FL

❧ ONE ROLY-POLY, TWO ROLY-POLY

January 1961 was cold and snowy in Pennsylvania. Before going out to play in the snow, my brother David, 2, and I got bundled up in our bright red winter wear. My guess is that our parents, Frank and Rose, dressed us in red so we would be easy to find.

SUSAN LYONS DIETRICH · MONACA, PA

❝

I started turning our backyard into an ice rink in 1971 so my son Ken could work on his slap shots.

GREG LOPATKA
DOWNERS GROVE, IL

« BRING ON THE SNOW

My little brother Kim and I received a Silver Streak sled for Christmas in 1952. Whenever it snowed, we would go out sledding. Growing up in Denver, Colorado, we had so much fun with that sled and our round fiberglass saucer sled, too.

JULIE MANN · CENTENNIAL, CO

TO BE A KID AGAIN

BROADWAY BABY

As many girls were persuaded to do in the 1950s, I started tap-dancing lessons when I was 4. Our costumes could have anything from big bows to Carmen Miranda-style fruit baskets that we had to balance on our heads while tapping away. After seven years, I traded my tap shoes for my next musical adventure, piano lessons. While I enjoy seeing different styles of dance on TV, I'll take a simple tap routine to "Stardust" anytime.

LINDA KNOX · BATAVIA, NY

FLUFFY COMPANION

The Groom brothers, Jeff, myself and Joe, pose with our first pet, Lambert, in 1959. Our father was a butcher and would bring home different animals from time to time.

GREG GROOM
COLUMBUS, OH

CUTE AS A BUTTON »

My mother, Susie, 2, leans in to blow out the candles on her birthday cake at home in Ashtabula, Ohio.

CLAIRE BURKHOLDER
GENEVA, OH

ALL THE FRILLS ❧

My mother, Gertrude Hear, wore this white dress with eyelet ruffles and a matching hair bow, tights and shoes when she made both her communion and confirmation in May 1921.

GERTRUDE BUMILLER
KEANSBURG, NJ

My grandparents' farm in Kemper County, Mississippi, was the magical place I spent my summer holidays every year. One summer, when I was 12, I had a pet rooster.

JIM LUKE
PICAYUNE, MS

Through Mrs. See's Eyes

Small kindnesses loom large as life plows on.

The winter I was in eighth grade in the early 1970s, a lot of snow dropped on our town of Kasilof, Alaska. That was fine by me, for my father would let me plow our 1,000-foot private road with the little John Deere 1010 dozer. His only stipulation: I also had to plow the drive of our nearest neighbor, Mrs. See, a 75-year-old retired teacher.

The thrill of clattering around on the John Deere was ample compensation, but it couldn't compare to Mrs. See insisting in her charming English accent that I join her for "tea and biscuits with Johnny Carson" when I finished.

Her father had come from England to seek his fortune during the Klondike Gold Rush, but he'd struck it rich in a different way. "I found all the gold I needed in your mother," he often told his daughter.

The plowing done, I'd find Mrs. See waiting inside with a hug and a compliment—"What a fine young man you are, Mike"—before she led me past her sleeping husband to a recliner next to a TV tray, where she'd set the teapot, cups, bowl of sugar, pitcher of milk and plate of Lorna Doone cookies. She always tried to give me $5 for plowing and I always refused. Truth be told, I looked forward to watching *The Tonight Show* as much as driving the plow because we didn't have a TV

at home. After a half-hour or so, I'd thank her, hug her goodbye and clank back up the hill on the old John Deere as she watched from her doorway.

The next winter, her husband, Toby, died. In our little community on the Kenai Peninsula, being a gravedigger was a great honor. I was gratified when Mrs. See asked me to be one of the four gravediggers for Toby.

On that cold March day, Mrs. See's son and one of her nephews hacked at the ground with picks and shovels. They were sturdy men, both fishermen, but the first 3 feet of earth were frozen solid and came away in small pieces. I waited my turn to dig with Brock, the Sees' 17-year-old grandson.

When we finally finished, Mrs. See's son said a simple prayer and handed each of the other gravediggers an envelope with a new $100 bill. We understood that it wasn't a payment, but a token of her appreciation.

Although I am not as old as Mrs. See was when we watched TV together, I am closer to her age now than I am to the teenager I was then. Because of her, I learned to say thank you often and to appreciate the best in people.

Thank you, Mrs. See, for having made my world a better place.

MIKE CORDLE · BREMERTON, WA

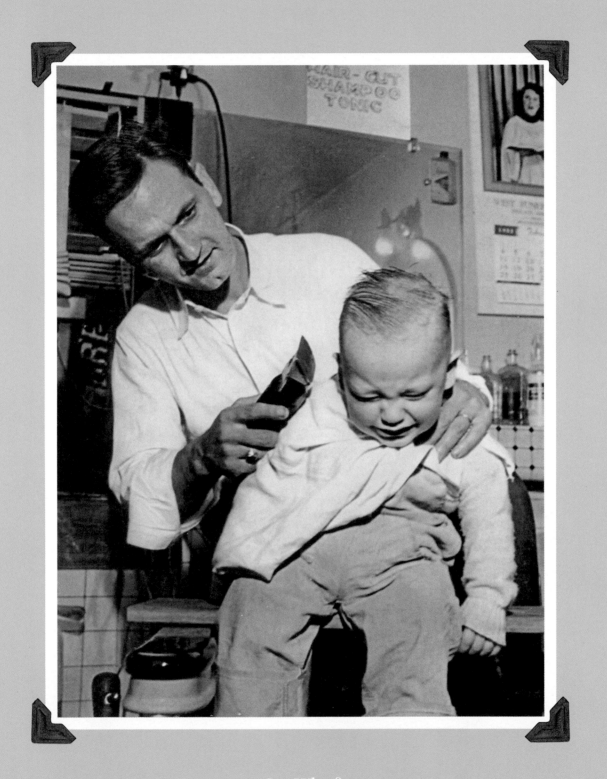

Cut What?

Barber Douglas Higgins gave me my first haircut in 1951, when I was 11 months old. My dad, John Wood Sr., captured my reaction like the pro he was—he worked as a staff photographer for *The Richmond News Leader* in Richmond, Virginia.

J.C. WOOD · MECHANICSVILLE, VA

CHAPTER 2

....

ALL IN THE FAMILY

They are our best friends, the first ones
we turn to for a kind word or a quick hug,
and they're always good for a laugh!

MAY · 55

Simple Pleasures

Bruce (left) and I, 15 and 18, hang out with our
sister Phyllis, 5, on a trip to a tiny island in Lake Huron
in 1949. This was our mother's favorite picture of us.

H. CLARK DEAN · GLENCOE, IL

Many generations of Reminders gathered for a celebration when this photo was taken in 1942.

Remember the Reminders

A now thriving community recalls a family's past.

F riday, June 26, 1942. The U.S. had been fighting in World War II since December, and the Battle of Midway, just a few weeks earlier, had marked a much-needed victory and a turning point for U.S. troops fighting in the Pacific.

On that particular summer day, my maternal ancestors gathered at Geauga Lake in Aurora, Ohio, for a family photograph. They were celebrating the 65th wedding anniversary of George Reminder Sr. and Genevieve Schall, my great-great-great grandparents.

Both were then 84 and had been born into families that immigrated to the U.S. from Germany in the early 1800s. At the time, they had 13 children, 40 grandchildren, and 29 great-grandchildren.

George Sr. reigned as the patriarch of the Reminder family from the late 1800s through the 1940s. However, it would be his son, my great-great grandfather George Jr., along with younger brothers Frank and Clement and their friend Peter Grimm Sr., who would plant the seeds of Reminderville, Ohio.

Reminderville is a village at the northeastern tip of Summit County in northeast Ohio, and one of three locations in Ohio where four counties—Cuyahoga, Geauga, Portage and

The village began more than 60 years ago with a population of a couple of hundred residents.

Summit—meet at a single point. Until the 1960s, a two-lane road, Orchard Street, was the only way to get to or out of Reminderville.

The village began more than 60 years ago with a population of a couple of hundred residents. Now more than 4,000 people call the place home.

Earlier in the 1920s, George Jr., Frank, and Clement had purchased lots where they built summer cottages to relax, fish and have picnics away from the city.

The first permanent and year-round resident of the area, Peter Grimm Sr., moved to the area from Cleveland in 1931 with his wife, Emma, and daughter Lillian, 2, and they lived at the end of a meandering road.

In the years after the 1929 stock market crash, the Reminder brothers converted their summer cottages into permanent homes. Settling into the new location, George continued to work in Cleveland at a manufacturing company and raise chickens in his garage, Frank became a farmer, and Clement managed a business.

The land, originally part of Twinsburg Township, began being referred to as Reminderville because of who lived there. Soon even truck drivers called the area Reminderville to prevent accidental deliveries to the nearby town of Twinsburg.

In time, George found lots where his children could build, and by the 1950s, the area had become a mecca for relaxed living outside Cleveland. Then serious talks began about Reminderville becoming its very own entity.

In 1955, following decades of development and hard work, the Village of Reminderville was made official. Clement was elected the town's first mayor in April of that year, though his tenure lasted only one year after illness forced him to step down.

Meanwhile, George worked with both the Summit County engineer and a landowner to build an alternate road into town. Glenwood Drive opened in 1962 and linked Reminderville to Liberty Road in Twinsburg, a huge convenience for residents and the surrounding communities.

More than 60 years later, Reminderville is a thriving community and has annexed more land from Twinsburg Township. The earliest summer cottages are gone, but the year-round homes built in the 1930s still stand.

But for the efforts of my great-great-grandfather, his brothers, and their friend, Reminderville would not exist today. They championed this town and created one of the finest communities I know in northeast Ohio.

SAM GEORGEVICH · TWINSBURG, OH

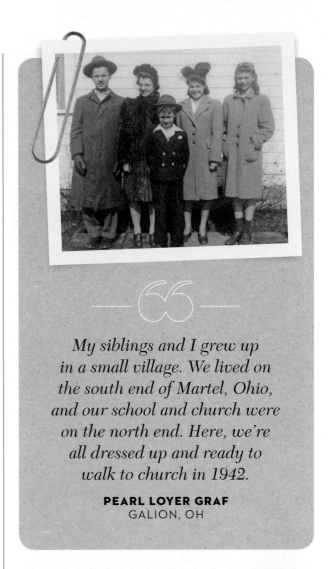

My siblings and I grew up in a small village. We lived on the south end of Martel, Ohio, and our school and church were on the north end. Here, we're all dressed up and ready to walk to church in 1942.

PEARL LOYER GRAF
GALION, OH

SHOPPING CLOSE TO HOME
We lived above the local Seavey's grocery store in Windham in 1942. My mom, Mary, holds my younger brother, Russell, and our neighbor, Gary Worthley, sits on the stoop next to her. Dad made my tricycle's storage box so I could haul things.
GEORGE HALL · WINDHAM, ME

What a ride! Mark toboggans with his mother, Martie Villwock, and their hunting dog Shatzi.

Mountain Expeditions

That regular trek to the snow was the
high point of the year.

Every year in the early '70s, my sisters and I looked forward to our trip to Big Bear Mountain, California. Growing up in Orange County, we were unaccustomed to snow or heights, so when we were driving the winding mountain road, our mother, Martie, would start white-knuckling the dashboard. She whined to Dad at every curve with a long, drawn-out, "Oh, Don, be careful!"

Her matter-of-life-or-death reaction made the otherwise dull drive quite exciting. At the same time, my sister Debbie and I would enter another round of the great American child's game Stop Touching Me, also known as Mom, He/She Won't Stop Touching Me. We'd finish the trip with rousing games of How Much Longer? and Are We There Yet?

Whenever we ventured up the mountain, within minutes we would beg our parents to stop for at least one sled ride or an impromptu snowball fight to tide us over for the rest of the drive. Heaven forbid if it threatened to snow. Then we'd race off the mountain for fear of getting caught in a blizzard. I was 30 before I actually saw snow fall.

Before heading home, we'd pile snow on the car as proof of our winter-weather excursion. We shared the spoils of our victory over the mountain with the whole neighborhood.

MARK VILLWOCK CORREY · NORTH TUSTIN, CA

Bicycle of Champions

It took a whole lot of cereal to win that prize.

———

My dad, Peter Hauterbrook, was 11 in 1947 when he entered a contest at a grocery store in Green Bay, Wisconsin. Whoever collected the most Wheaties box tops would receive a new bicycle from the store. Young Peter was set on winning, and as the family story goes, his goal caused a ruckus at home.

His Aunt Verna worked in the kitchen at the county hospital in Green Bay at the time and—guess what?—they served Wheaties for breakfast. In those days, there were no bulk packages, only regular-sized cereal boxes.

Verna collected as many box tops as she could, and by the time the contest ended, my father had won by a landslide.

My great-aunt's version of the events had a little more flavorful language. She referred to Dad as the little stinker and emphasized that the reason he won was because she helped him. She loved to give him the business, and she loved to spoil us kids.

Aunt Verna died and the bike is long gone. But we still have all the wonderful stories she told us about the escapades of that little stinker.

PETER HAUTERBROOK II · LUXEMBURG, WI

Young Peter was set on winning, and as the family story goes, his goal caused a ruckus at home.

Collecting box tops was the key to Peter's new bike.

Standing on the dock with his grandfather Julius Jensen and a big fish, Mike was 2.

Second Time Around

He found he'd cast back to the spot Grandpa loved.

———

My parents and grandparents liked to vacation on lakes in northern Minnesota and Wisconsin. They also loved to catch and eat fish. So when I was young I could hardly wait for my grandpa to take me fishing.

When I got older, I couldn't remember where the photo of Grandpa and me standing on a dock was taken. But as I stared at the picture, I noticed a name on the side of the boat next to me. Looking more closely, I recognized the words "Rest Point," but didn't see any other identifying marks.

I mentioned this to my sister, and she told me she thought she had the same picture in a photo album our mother had given her. After finding the picture, she called to tell me that the writing on the back said: "Rest Point Resort, Bone Lake WI, June 1941."

I could hardly believe it. My wife and I have a park model trailer in that very resort about 20 yards from the cabin in the photo. The cabin has been remodeled, so the outside looks different, but inside it remains quite rustic.

We have a beautiful view of the lake, and I often gaze at the cabin I stayed in so many years ago with fond memories.

J. MICHAEL HYLAND · WOODVILLE, WI

'I am Spartacus'

Hollywood star inspires Mom's act of defiance.

E very small town in America had a tiny movie theater in the 1950s. In our hamlet of Hessville, Indiana, it was the Ace on Kennedy Avenue, sandwiched in between Janc Drugs and Vierk's Furniture. About 3 miles away, downtown Hammond had big theaters, including the Parthenon, but I'd never been to any of them. That is, not until 1960—when a magnificent event occurred in our family.

Going to the movies was rare for the Goodsons because we had more children than cash. But it became easier once my sister Barb married, brother Bill joined the Navy, and sister Kay started hanging around with Mell.

One afternoon, while Dad was at work, our mother, Nancy, told my sister Wanda and me to dress up. Mom even put on makeup, which she rarely did. As we walked down Kennedy, I asked her where we were going.

"To the show," she replied. When I looked over at the Ace, she added, "not that one."

We hopped on the bus to Hammond and got off at the Parthenon, where the huge 1920s-era marquee practically shouted the current feature: *Spartacus*, starring Kirk Douglas.

Inside, there were at least a thousand red velour seats, with more in a long balcony that stretched in an elegant curve across the theater. Every inch of trim was painted gold, and statues of Greek gods hung on the walls. The screen was easily three times larger than the Ace's. I thought, *This is gonna be good.*

And it was. Wanda and I loved the movie. But we wondered why Mom had done this. It was so unlike her. She didn't talk on the way home, but when we got off the bus she turned to us: "Let this be our own little secret, all right? We don't need to mention this to Dad."

At home we changed back into our everyday clothes and Mom removed her makeup. Dad never suspected a thing.

Much later, we figured it out: Mom had a mad crush on Kirk Douglas, but Dad had refused to take her to the movie. So she used some of her household money to go anyway, in what proved

Nancy staged a one-woman revolt to see Kirk Douglas on the big screen.

to be one of a few small acts of independence in her 44 years of marriage to a domineering man. Our trip to Hammond was one of her Spartacus moments, when she identified with the rebel slave of the film.

Mom's final act of rebellion came when she died. In her will she stipulated that she was to be buried next to her mother in Illinois, and not by her husband in Indiana. Nancy may not have had the most words in their marriage, but she certainly had the last.

MICHAEL GOODSON · HIGHLAND, IN

Living off the land was a natural choice for Ralph and Nancy Bell, pictured with John, James and Martha in about 1965. Ralph Jr. and daughter Nancy came along later.

Dinner Plans Changed

Getting close to their food gave them a new perspective.

To get away from a stressful job as a school superintendent in the Southern California mountains, Dad retired and my parents, Ralph and Nancy Bell, moved to the San Juan Islands in Washington in about 1978. They wanted to live close to nature, growing their own vegetables, raising fruit and nut trees, and being self-sufficient. They bought a boat to catch fish.

They found a 6½-acre plot across from a wild bird preserve. It had a well, barn, chicken coop and corral, along with huge areas for plantings and a forest at the rear edge. They bought two horses, several chickens, four lambs and a goat.

And they raised three beautiful fat turkeys. One was intended for Thanksgiving, one for Christmas and one for Easter. They bought a large freezer to keep the birds after processing.

Just before Thanksgiving, they prepped a picnic table to process all three turkeys. The plan was that once the birds were killed, Mom, Dad and daughter Nancy would pluck the feathers and clean the carcasses. When it was time to pluck, however, they couldn't go on.

"How can we possibly eat the turkeys that ran up to greet us every morning?" Mom asked. "How can we eat the chickens who lay eggs for us every day?"

We buried the turkeys in the forest and had Thanksgiving without one.

And that is how my parents lived the rest of their six years on the island. They had such reverence for life that they could hardly kill a single living creature. The sheep who kept the grass trimmed became pets. One ewe died giving birth to twins, so we bottle-fed her lambs as they sat on our laps. When they were old enough to feed themselves, the lambs would come to the back door and call out *maaa, maaa, maaa.*

The chickens died of old age. Our family did catch and eat fish, though Mom always found it distressing to clean them.

When their remote location became too tricky for my parents to navigate, they resettled in Edmonds, Washington. But they never lost their appreciation for nature.

MARTHA C. KARR · GIG HARBOR, WA

LITTLE CONVENIENCES

Small appliances were a big help when entertaining.

1950 »

Dormeyer On the Job

The products by this Chicago-based competitor to Sunbeam were better designed and more durable, but they were expensive and lacked cute, memorable names. For instance, its top line stand mixer was the Food-Fixer; Sunbeam's was the Mixmaster. In 1960, Dormeyer was sold to an audio equipment maker, where poor leadership led to its insolvency.

« 1955

Class Up Your Instant

Nescafé joined with Pyrex to promote this attractive coffee server—and enlisted etiquette guru Emily Post to extol the virtue of always having piping hot coffee ready when guests come over. Who cares if the "company coffee" is instant (and tastes like it)? It looks fabulous.

Sisters Amanda and Selma Hanson wear stylish hats, suggesting they were attending a special occasion. By the late 1800s, American women were spending $100 million on Easter hats. In today's money, that's more than $90 per woman.

If These Photos Could Talk

Vintage images unlock stories about the past.

My husband Rick's mother, Aleah Bell Coffman, was 18 when she married Gordon Wenzler and moved from her home in Kansas to Milwaukee, Wisconsin, leaving behind her mother, Amanda; father, Walter; sister, Loretta; and brothers Clarence and Burdett.

Loretta was 15 years older than Aleah Bell, but the sisters were very close. Loretta even picked her sister's name, which Aleah Bell disliked all her life.

Aleah Bell met Gordy in early 1945 when he was stationed in Manhattan, Kansas, with the Army Air Corps. A high school senior at the time, Aleah Bell

worked at a gas station in the nearby town of Fort Riley. Gordy used to joke about her work overalls.

The couple married in December that year just before Gordy got out of the service, and they went to Milwaukee to live with his parents and sister before moving into their own house down the street.

Rick and I began dating while attending the University of Wisconsin-Stevens Point. He showed me these and other wonderful photos and told me many stories about his family. Uncle Burdett ran a flooring and tile business in Kansas, while Uncle Clarence joined the Navy during World War II and

The 1904 wedding portrait of Rick's grandparents Walter and Amanda Coffman is likely a cabinet card, a very thin photograph mounted on a 4-by-6-inch card, popular in the late 1800s. The backdrop was one of several they could have chosen at the studio. The couple's clothing and hairstyles are indicative of the early 1900s.

Brothers Clarence and Burdett Coffman are dressed in a style common until the late 19th and early 20th centuries. Boys wore dresses until the time of breeching—roughly until toilet training—when they officially graduated to pants.

When I rang the bell, an older man opened the door and scooped me into his arms.

afterward moved to Los Angeles, California, to work for Lockheed.

Clarence loved his little sis, Aleah Bell, and used to visit her in Milwaukee each summer. Fishing was his passion; he had a tradition during his annual trip to Wisconsin of buying a new fishing hat and lures, and at the end of the vacation, leaving the hat at the restaurant where they went for breakfast.

I met Clarence in 1971, when my dad and I, running an errand, stopped by Rick's house on our way from Kaukauna to Kenosha. When I rang the bell, an older man opened the door and scooped me into his arms. Thank goodness Rick had prepared me. "Oh, hi," I said. "You must be Uncle Clarence."

INA WENZLER · PORT WASHINGTON, WI

Just a Spoonful of Sugar

Siblings shared a sweet secret about
the school basement.

Rex Ashby, my dad, was a hardworking man in blue overalls who raised nine children—seven girls and two boys—during the Depression. In his prime, he was a jack-of-all-trades and an inventor. At one time, he was custodian at the high school in Hover, Washington, on the Columbia River, about 12 miles east of Kennewick.

But what I remember most about my father is his passion and skill for candymaking. Divinity, penuche and cocoa sour cream fudge were his favorites, and Dad's reputation as a candymaker lasted his whole life.

While stoking the coal furnace in the basement of the schoolhouse where he worked, he would wait for the fire to die down, pull out a bag of ingredients he'd brought from home and, just before the furnace needed stoking again, start cooking his confections. He held the mixture over the hot coals using a pot with a long piece of wood attached to the handle.

When we sniffed the aroma of fudge or popcorn coming through the ventilation system, my siblings and I knew Dad was busy mixing up a treat. We would sneak down to the basement between classes, sometimes bringing guests with us.

We moved when Dad worked in the Portland, Oregon, shipyards for a time, eventually returning to Kennewick. Here, Dad graduated to bigger and better candymaking techniques. He bought an enormous marble slab and a candy thermometer so he could gauge the temperature of the boiling mass of candy. Once it reached the critical stage, he would throw his concoction onto the cool slab and swirl it until it cooled and set up at just the right consistency.

I have to admit there were times when I tired of homemade fudge and yearned for the store-bought candy bars we got at Christmas. But over the years, my feelings have changed.

As my sisters and brothers and I had children of our own, we often visited Grandpa Rex and Grandma Martha, and a tradition was born. The first order of business when we arrived—find the fudge. This brought everyone joy. That memory still rests warm on my heart and the hearts of my children.

ROSEMARY ASHBY KINSFATHER
REDONDO BEACH, CA

Rex and his dog, Lucy, unwind on the front porch.

Vivid crests on Mari's charm bracelet mark her adventures with her family.

A HANDY GUIDE TO THE CITIES OF EUROPE

TRAVELING IN THE LATE 1940s AND early '50s with our parents was exciting for my brother, Gerry, and me. At the time, Dad worked for the American Red Cross and was attached to various branches of the military all over the world.

In the late spring of 1956 we were living in Long Beach, California. I was in fourth grade and looking forward to the summer, when Dad came home with exciting news. We were moving to Bordeaux, France!

There was a dizzying flurry of planning, preparation—including selling our house—and packing for our overseas trip that quickly followed. Meanwhile, Dad went on ahead to France to find us a place to live.

As soon as the school year ended, our dauntless mom took Gerry, 8, and me, 9, to Santa Ana, California, where we caught a train to go across country. We spent more than a week traveling, stopping to visit relatives along the way, before reaching New York, where we got

on a military transport ship for a six-day voyage across the Atlantic to Bremerhaven, Germany. There we again boarded a train, this time to Paris, where Dad met us, loaded all of our luggage into a car and took us to our new home in Bordeaux.

Though Mom and Dad loved to travel through Europe with us, they had to watch their expenses carefully on Dad's limited salary, so we couldn't buy a lot of souvenirs. Instead, they gave me a bracelet and offered to buy me a charm at each of the cities we visited.

Many cities and towns had charms that were in the design of their crests, so I always looked forward to the next trip and the possibility of adding a new location to my bracelet.

Now whenever I wear it, I think of the wonderful opportunities that our parents provided us and the memories we shared. My brother and I still love to travel. We can trace our wanderlust directly to our parents' adventurous spirit and their desire to give their children experiences that few others had.

MARI PAGE · FOUNTAIN VALLEY, CA

LASTING BONDS

ANY GIVEN SUNDAY

Every Sunday, my parents and I started the day by going to Mass. After that, whenever the Chicago Cubs had a doubleheader, we were off to Wrigley Field.

My parents are both from Italy. My dad was a butcher and would never allow me to have hot dogs at the park. Instead, my mom fixed Italian chicken with fruit, vegetables and, of course, wine for our ballpark picnics. People around us always wanted to know what we were eating.

GIOVANNA OLIVIERI-LEWIS
CINCINNATI, OH

OUT FOR A STROLL

My Aunt Rose didn't have children, so I'd stay with her in Chicago for a week at a time. I loved playing with her jewelry. I'm in the middle; cousin Barbara (Czeska) Bromberak is holding my hand.
MARGO SHAFRANSKI SIERACKI
JOLIET, IL

CITY KIDS
My sons, Anthony, left, and Richard and Michael, standing at right, played with neighbor kids in the '50s in East Cambridge, Massachusetts. I used the red Ford for my plaster and tile-setting business.
MARIO J. CELLA · DELRAY BEACH, FL

LASTING BONDS

⌃ LIFE OF LEISURE
I made these leisure suits for Mike, 7, Aaron, 3, and Steve, 5, back in 1976. The outfits were cute, although I couldn't say I was sorry to see the style change. Today, the boys can't believe we had them wear those things.
ROBERTA HALDIMAN
SOUTH WAYNE, WI

SEA BREEZES ⌄
We loved to take annual jaunts with our daughters Ann and Lani. In 1964, we stopped in beautiful Monterey on California's central coast.
MERRY FLANAGAN · ST. PAUL, MN

« WEDDING SHOWER
When I was growing up we visited my Grandmother Alma, whom we called Mamaw, at least once a week—you were always guaranteed a good meal and wonderful memories. All the ladies in this 1954 photo are related to each other in some way. Mamaw is standing in the left corner, and my mother, Beverly, stands second from right in the back row.
PATRICIA RUSSELL
EVANSVILLE, IN

THREE OF A KIND »

I dressed my three sons—Gary, 4, Greg, 3, and Glenn, 5—alike for this picture taken in 1954.

JOAN HERBST
BOYERTOWN, PA

> *My son Dean, 8, strummed a guitar nearly as big as him while my daughter Judy, 3, sat on the sidewalk in 1963.*
>
> **MARIE METHENY MIDDLETON**
> RIVERDALE, CA

⌃ AFTERNOON DRIVE

I often played underfoot at my parents' bakery in Ashland, Oregon, in the late 1930s. On Sunday afternoons my parents didn't work and, after lunch, the family would pile into the car for a country drive. Here my brother Fred and I, then 12 and 8, stand near the car with our mother, keeping warm in our dapper hats and fur-collared jackets.

BILL BUEHLING · DUNSMUIR, CA

Approved for Flight

His drive for independence led to a soaring career.

W hen I became a teenager, my family moved from Greensboro, North Carolina, to Coral Gables, Florida. I saved for college by washing windows and cars and mowing the lawn at my dad's real estate office in Kendall.

We kept a power mower and an old bike in the office garage, and when I finished mowing, I'd hop on the bike and check out the new area. Within a mile of the office I discovered a small grass-strip airport. I went there every Saturday to watch the flight school instructors teach students to fly.

One Saturday, the flight school manager offered to take me for a plane ride on a weekday afternoon if my folks approved. Not only did my dad say yes, he wanted to come with me. My father had flown airplanes during World War II, and this was a way for us to bond.

After arranging for someone to mind his office on a Tuesday afternoon, he picked me up at school and we drove to Brown's Airport for what became my first flying lesson. I left the airport that day with a pilot's logbook and my first entry, Sept. 13, 1955.

On the way home I found myself suddenly in a new kind of father-son relationship. Now we were two guys talking about flying. I soloed in November 1955 and got my student pilot's license before I got my driver's license.

Eventually I flew for the Air Force, commercial and private aviation companies, and the aerospace industry, which came with an ID badge and unlimited access to Cape Canaveral.

DAN JONES · LAKE WALES, FL

Caught Left-Handed

My sweetheart, Pete Kimiecik, shares his love of fishing with his son
Chris and daughter Lynn in Chester, New York, in 1984. A large
percentage of kids in the area fish left-handed because of Pete.

CLARE KIRKWOOD · FLORIDA, NY

CHAPTER 3

······························

TRUE LOVE

Sometimes we choose sweethearts and sometimes they choose us, leading to exciting encounters and lasting romance.

As the Camera Rolls

One of the first couples married on television were my mom
and dad, Rita and Irving Litt. The show, which aired in 1950 on
KLAC-TV in Los Angeles, California, was called "Wedding Bells."
They celebrate their anniversary on Aug. 26.

RICHARD LITT • SHERMAN OAKS, CA

Honeymoon bound, Lynn and Robert wed on March 1, 1969.

That Bus Trip Changed Everything

She had what no one else had.

■

A group of residents from the singles apartment complex where I lived in 1968 decided to take a weekend ski trip. We scheduled a bus to transport us from Dallas, Texas, to Ruidoso, New Mexico. I was three years out of college, and had no idea I was going to meet the love of my life that February.

During the hourslong bus ride, Lynn McDonald and her four girlfriends cleverly sat in the front of the bus. They picked the spot right next to the keg of beer because the guys made frequent visits there. I tried to get Lynn to come to the back of the bus where we were having an impromptu party, but she refused. Her friend Ann, however, jumped at the opportunity.

Later I invited Lynn to a Saturday night party, but she insisted that I get all her friends to come as well. Lynn and I slow-danced at the party that evening, and I continued to find ways to spend time with her on the slopes. She just had something special no one else had.

When I asked her to ride home with me on the bus, she hesitated, possibly thinking Ann and I had something going. I knew that convincing Lynn to ride home with me would be my biggest sell job.

Clockwise from left: Skiing in New Mexico, Lynn dressed for the conditions. She sips from Robert's wine bag. The couple got married the following year.

She agreed, and it was wonderful. She was so enjoyable to talk with. Something special was happening between us.

We stopped for a buffet dinner on the way home. I wanted to pay for her meal, but she refused. I thought to myself, *She'll buy this one, but I'll buy her meals for the rest of her life.*

We shared a blanket on the bus and went out the next night, the following night and the night after that.

I was rather naive at the time, but when a friend said to me, "I hear you're in love," I finally realized, *Wow! That's what this is.*

Lynn was and is the only girl to whom I've ever said, "I love you." After a year together and having many good times and parties with family and friends, we were married. We've been happy together ever since.

ROBERT J. MURRAY · CARROLLTON, TX

That commander knew best: Hark was at Pat's side for her TV spot and later for their wedding.

The Reluctant Escort

For this Seabee, it paid to follow orders.

Each year, as a way to celebrate the anniversary of the Navy Construction Battalion (Seabees), our Seabee center at Port Hueneme held a contest to crown a young lady as the queen of the military ball.

In the weeks leading up to the big gala, each contestant was escorted to various functions at the base, by either an enlisted person or an officer, and one of the functions involved appearing on a television show filmed in Santa Barbara. These events gave everyone who'd be selecting the queen an opportunity to see the contestants before casting their votes.

As an instructor on the base in 1956, I was rarely asked to be an escort. The organizers did their best to match up the young women with escorts who were close to their age and had shared interests. But it was often a difficult task, because many of the Seabee escorts were either very young or married.

On one occasion, the committee was working hard to find someone to take a contestant named Pat Swaney to her TV appearance—and they landed on me. Except I was teaching a class that I couldn't leave.

They asked me twice to escort Miss Swaney. Each time I said no. But it happened that Miss Swaney was the commanding officer's secretary—and the CO was not pleased with my persistent refusals.

The third time I was approached about escorting her, it was by the CO himself. He ordered me to put on my dress blues, get a car from the car pool and take the young woman to the TV station.

On the way to the studio, I was fuming for having to leave my class. But by the time we were on TV, I had settled down and started to enjoy myself. In fact, Pat and I were getting along very well.

After that first impromptu date, I saw her every day for the next 90 days, at which time we tied the knot. Looking back, those were the best orders I ever received—they led to more than 60 years of love and togetherness.

HARK KETELS · CAMARILLO, CA

Prim and Proper, Forever

Following protocol was the only way to date.

When I left school in California to return to Mexico in 1956, I was 21 and went to work in my father's fishing cannery. I swore to all my relatives and friends at the time that I would remain a bachelor until I was 30.

Then one day, I spotted Mary, 19, at a traditional Mexican afternoon dance in Ensenada. She was beautiful, poised and slim, with a long brown ponytail. To say I was smitten would be an understatement. But she was with a male partner, so I could not interfere. Proper social protocol in Mexico in the 1950s demanded formality.

I learned that Mary was working as a teller in a bank, Banco Mexicano de Occidente. Oddly enough, I thought I had seen her at a different bank. The mystery was solved when I found out Mary had a twin sister, Teresa, who worked at the other bank.

Another dilemma confronted me then: I couldn't just walk up to Mary and ask for a date, as that was considered too forward. So I persuaded a mutual acquaintance of ours to introduce us. From that moment on, I courted Mary, but always with a chaperone—her twin, Teresa—present.

Three weeks after we met, I swallowed my sworn statement about bachelorhood and proposed. Because Mary's father had died in a plane crash, my parents formally asked her mother for her hand.

From top: Ariel and Mary traveled to Mexico City and Acapulco, Mexico, for their honeymoon. For 44 years, they hugged each other daily and celebrated the good times.

We were married in Ensenada in 1958. Five years later, in 1963, we moved to San Diego. We had two children and eventually had five grandchildren. Mary worked as a supervisor at a savings and loan association, and I worked for the California state government until 1998, when I retired.

One summer day the following year, Mary was diagnosed with an incurable immune disorder. The doctor gave her at most two years, and I became her caregiver. She was a trouper and fought her illness with everything she had until she died three years later, on Aug. 18, 2002.

Is it possible that love continues to grow more with time? It did for Mary and me.

Does love end when one's soul mate dies? After 44 years together, we were inseparable. A plaque I gave Mary many years ago sums up our life together: We are one love forever.

ARIEL MORALES
EL CAJON, CA

Happy couple Caryl and LaVerne made a vow to work together the rest of their lives.

Traffic-Stopping Proposal
Saying three important words meant a lot.

R iding home from the grocery store one day, Caryl, acting as co-pilot, reminded me to "sic 'em" when we needed to turn. After spending four years together, we'd developed a private language all our own.

Then suddenly, in the midst of traffic, he began talking about us. This was a bit unusual because I normally had to prime him with questions before he offered an opinion on anything. But today was different. He was talking about how well we suited each other. Not surprisingly, I found myself silently agreeing with everything he said.

After a few more sentences, it occurred to me that he was really talking about getting

married—right there in the middle of Liberty Street traffic. Since my hands were gripping the wheel, it took me a while to clarify my thoughts. Finally, with my eyes bulging out of their sockets, I asked, "Are you saying you want to get married?"

"Yeah, I guess so," he replied.

Once we got to my place, we sat down for a heart-to-heart talk. "Caryl," I said, "give me three good reasons why you think we should get married."

"Three?"

I rolled my eyes. "OK, make it two, but this is a test."

"Well, we get along really well."

"Yes, and...?"

"We don't like to be alone."

I shook my head in response. "Wrong answers. You have one more chance."

Then his eyes opened wide, and he seemed to figure it out. "Oh, I love you," he said. "But you already know that."

I shook my head again at his difficulty in getting to the right answer. I wanted him to stew in his own juices for a while, so I told him I needed to pray about it.

"Sure," he said. "I already have. Take your time."

That was Saturday.

At church the next morning, I got an answer to my prayer. The subject for the day was "How to Improve a Marriage." As you can imagine, I listened carefully to every word. It seemed too coincidental not to be an answer to my prayer. That afternoon, I used the time to point out to Caryl the difficulties we might face as a married couple: our age difference of 20 years (he was 94 and I was 74), his great love for his former wife, health issues, personality differences and financial problems that might arise. He also knew why I was extra cautious about men and had been single for a total of 38 long years.

He listened considerately, and we spent the afternoon discussing all the "what-ifs."

Then I drove him home to his son's house. We didn't talk much along the way, but as he turned in the seat to get out of the car I hugged him from behind, a bit longer than usual. Then I whispered in his ear, "Yes!"

He quickly turned around and said, "I figured you didn't want to."

"I know," I said. "I just needed to hear you say those wonderful words. I couldn't live through another loveless marriage."

Again he told me he loved me, to which I responded that I loved him, too, and he was my forever sweetheart.

Next came the much harder part—making it work. Fortunately we both were old enough to know what we were doing and that there would be obstacles ahead. But the best part was that we could lean on each other's strengths and meet the hard times together.

The year 2008 started out like gangbusters for us. What a real joy it was not to live alone anymore. Our new place—a manufactured home in a gated community—was perfect for our joyful home-based honeymoon. For three years after that, he took care of me and I took care of him. Those were the best three years of my life.

LAVERNE WINEGARDNER
KEIZER, OR

TWICE LOVED

JUST OUT OF THE AIR FORCE IN 1962, I WAS skating at the local roller rink in my hometown of Newhall, California, when a pretty dark-haired girl came in and started skating alone. I was a bit shy but found myself talking to her. I learned that her name was Carol Moss. She was 18 and had just moved to Newhall from Tennessee.

We dated steadily for the next 2½ years. We were in love but, to my surprise, when I asked her to marry me, she said no. She told me she was too young to get married. So we parted in 1964 with hurt feelings.

I later married, but lost my wife in 2013. The following year I visited Newhall with my buddy John Bullock. It was a 480-mile trip from my home in St. Helena in Napa Valley to Newhall.

While in Newhall I found out that Carol still lived there and was divorced. We met the next day and had quite a reunion. Afterward, we talked on the phone every day and I drove down to visit her often. We were engaged in June 2015. I'm in love with her for the second time, and together we moved back to Tennessee. I am one lucky guy. She's terrific.

DARRYL CAMERON · COOKEVILLE, TN

After they met in the early '60s, Darryl and Carol spent all their time together.

Fourth from left, Paul graduated with honors from Noncommissioned Officers Academy training.

Service with a Smile

He walked into that diner—and right into her heart.

D o you believe in love at first sight? At one time, I didn't think it was possible, but my wife proved me wrong.

Let's turn the clock back to June 1963, when I was in the service and arrived at the Savanna Army Depot outside of Savanna, Illinois, along the upper Mississippi River. I had just spent a month on leave in Chicago, where my mother had died that May.

Sadly, I had not seen my mother for about three years because I had been stationed in Verdun, France, for a few years and in Germany before that. The Army gave me a compassionate reassignment to the Savanna depot, and after getting my mother's affairs all in order, I went to my new duty station.

I spent my first day on base getting to know some of the guys. When they asked if I'd like to go into town to get a bite to eat, I agreed to join them. I thought it might take away some of the sadness in my heart.

We sat in a booth at the News Stand, a cozy restaurant in a corner building of this quaint little town. As I was going over the menu, the waitress, a beautiful young woman named Charlene, noticed that I was the new guy in town. She immediately turned to her friend and co-worker Pat Haynes, pointed at me and said, "I'm going to marry that man."

She immediately turned to her friend and co-worker Pat Haynes,
pointed at me and said, "I'm going to marry that man."

Mind you, I had not yet seen Charlene. She smiled at me like an angel while taking my order. I have to admit, I didn't have a love-at-first-sight moment. But in the next few weeks, she took my heart and made me her guy.

We dated for almost a year. We were the perfect couple—an Army guy and a town girl. I used to tease her that the student enrollment at my high school in Chicago was more than twice the population of her small town.

She'd never been outside of the area, so I took her to Chicago to have a fun time and to meet my dad and some friends.

We decided to elope on April Fools' Day 1964. Looking back, that was the best day of my life.

Shortly after our son, Paul, was born, I received orders to go back to Germany. Charlene and Paul stayed in Savanna, but when my phone bills started eating up all my pay, I asked my first sergeant to bring my family over. On Paul's first birthday they arrived in Bremerhaven. That was the best tour ever because we could jump into the car and travel anywhere in Europe.

Thanks to the Army, I was able to bring Charlene with me to see many different places and have exciting adventures. We have been blessed with a son, a daughter, a granddaughter and many loyal friends.

All these years later I am very grateful that my beautiful wife trusted her love-at-first-sight moment.

PAUL MAYER · SAVANNA, IL

Top: Charlene and her new beau gaze tenderly at each other. Above: Still happy, Charlene and Paul have been married since 1964.

The couple met as first-graders. Ron is circled on the left and Lois is on the right.

It Was Meant to Be

Two dear friends glide easily into romance.

Lois and I met in 1951 when we both started first grade at Maple Elementary School in Springfield, Oregon. We also went to the same Sunday school. One Sunday at church, Lois pointed to me and told her mom, "That little boy is in my first-grade class at school." That was when we started our lifelong journey as friends.

The following year my parents moved out of town and I went to a different school. As it turned out, Lois' parents had moved to a small farm in the same area and, once again, we found ourselves going to the same school.

A year later, Lois and her parents moved back into town. Since my parents had moved back as well, we started third grade in the same school where we had been two years before. Throughout elementary, middle and high school, we always went to the same schools and even shared some classes together.

During all that time, we remained good friends. Based on our circle of classmates, we went on double dates together, dating each other's friends, but never each other.

Then one day just before high school graduation in 1963, we decided to go for a drive in the country together. We approached a local county park and, for some reason, I pulled off the road near the river. Just as we started talking, she reached over and gave me the best kiss I had ever had. The love that had been dormant all those years quickly began to bloom.

I got a job soon after graduation at Rosboro, a local plywood mill, where my dad worked. With my very first paycheck, I bought an engagement ring and asked Lois to marry me. Four months later we were a happy couple.

We have spent many wonderful years together and had the greatest adventures we could have ever imagined. With our family of children, grandchildren and great-grandchildren, we are still as much in love as ever.

RON COOPER · SPRINGFIELD, OR

TOGETHER FOR DECADES
1. When the duo started dating, Lois owned a 1955 Chevy. **2.** Coincidentally, Ron also owned a '55 Chevy. **3.** The couple got married about four months after graduation. **4.** Fifty-five years later, they celebrated their anniversary in Hawaii.

After his tour in Korea, Richard Steuart returned home and married Carol Bengston.

Worth the Effort

Dedication meant giving it one more try.

Dorothy and David had a fairy-tale romance—and a marriage that lasted 67 wonderful years.

After a two-day Thanksgiving visit home in 1948, I returned to West Point and told my roommates that I had met the girl I was going to marry. Her name was Carol Bengston, and she was the hospital nurse caring for my father after a minor hunting accident. I was halfway through my third year at the U.S. Military Academy and looking forward to graduation in June 1950.

During the early part of 1949, I made numerous phone calls to Carol asking for a date, but sadly, her answer was always no. West Point cadets thought that most girls would accept a date regardless of how they felt about the cadet, just to see the grounds. Not Carol. After months of getting negative responses, I accepted that our relationship would never blossom.

I graduated as a commissioned second lieutenant on June 6, 1950, along with 669 others. We had chosen our branch assignments (infantry, artillery, etc.) and initial duty stations months before, and were ready to ship out to various stations throughout the U.S.

Nineteen days later the North Koreans invaded South Korea. At the end of World War II, the U.S. had troops stationed in South Korea to support its army. These troops were soon fighting the North Korean forces. Many of my classmates were assigned to units engaged in those early months of the war. I had chosen the infantry, airborne, so was assigned to Fort Benning, Georgia, for parachute training. I then went to Fort Campbell, Kentucky, with the 11th Airborne Division. By November, I had volunteered for Korea with orders to depart in late December.

When I went home for a short leave in mid-December, I tried calling the woman I dated during graduation week. Alas, she now had other interests. I was heading out in a week and thought I'd give Carol another call. Initially, she said no. Then I asked, "How about the following night?" To my surprise, she agreed. I found out later that she was celebrating her birthday the first night.

We went out that next night and just about every night after. On Dec. 28, Carol joined my parents to see me off as I boarded a plane to the West Coast and on to Korea.

Carol and I exchanged many letters that year. I was wounded twice, completed my tour and returned home in December 1951. We were engaged on Jan. 1, 1952, and married on Jan. 12.

RICHARD STEUART · MELBOURNE, FL

A CRAZY IDEA

IN 1948 I WAS 18 AND DATING A girl named Lola Gorman from my high school. One night Lola and I decided to go swimming at the Hotel St. George in downtown Brooklyn, but we got lost and ended up at her grandmother's house. There, I was introduced to Lola's cousin Dorothy, a cute young woman wearing a black turtleneck sweater, black slacks and black penny loafers. She was living with her grandmother at the time.

After I met her, I couldn't get her out of my mind. Her grandmother told her I was the kind of boy she should go out with. When I broke up with her cousin, I decided to call Dorothy. She didn't want to go out with me at first, finally agreeing after many calls.

When I told her I was going to marry her, she said I was crazy. When I told my mother I had found the girl I was going to marry, she also said I was crazy. But things worked out and when we both turned 21, we had a beautiful wedding ceremony on Oct. 8, 1950. Dorothy died on May 17, 2017. I only hope that if there is a heaven, I will be with her again.

DAVID GROSS · BROOKLYN, NY

SWEET ROMANCE

IN THE BEGINNING

My first date with Roger Casseday in 1948 was on a night in the Alleghenies when the snow was so deep that he actually carried me through the drifts to the car. The way home was less eventful, except for the first of many kisses to come.

LOU CASSEDAY · NEWBURY, OH

SAVE THE LAST DANCE »

I went to my friend's, also a Judy, for a ride to the senior dance to find her mother had set Judy up on a date. So we all went together. It wasn't long before Bill, her date, asked me to dance, our first of many that night. Three and a half years later—in May 1965—Judy stood up at our wedding.

JUDY KELCH · RENO, NV

YOUNG LOVE ❥

I met Harold "Wavy" Dodge in 1943 while working at J.J. Newberry's five-and-dime. All the girls were trying to push their way into his heart, but I slipped in quietly and stayed there.

PHYLLIS DODGE FLOOD · WHITMAN, MA

> ❝
>
> *Caroline and I loved to travel and sail—always together, always in love. She was the best of first mates.*
>
> **RICHMOND TRIPP**
> DIGHTON, MA

SWEET ROMANCE

FOND MEMORIES
My parents, Tom and Dorothy Reardon, had a great time in New York City on their wedding trip. They settled in Missouri and raised 10 children. They were amazing parents; we remember them fondly at all of our family get-togethers.
PEGGY PHILLIPS
RAYMORE, MO

UNDER THE GYM LIGHTS
Sock hops at high school sealed our love, but it took another four years and a world war before Theresa and I married. Those years made our love closer and more precious.
BILL LIVINGSTONE
GOLETA, CA

FOR THE MODERN COUPLE

At midcentury, decor reflects new ways of living.

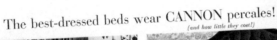

1953 »

Double Duty

Disguised beds had been around since 1885, when entrepreneur Sarah Goode got a U.S. patent—the first African-American woman to do so—for a folding cabinet sleeper. But these types of beds took off with the boom in rental housing in the 1950s.

« 1953

Tucked In and Tidy

Mass production all but eliminated embroidery and intricate detailing. Instead it produced crisp, unadorned sheets suited to the pared-down style of platform beds (top left). Modular layouts show the trend to combine both living and sleeping areas.

SWEET ROMANCE

WEDDING LINEUP
Starting as childhood sweethearts, my mother and father were married in 1928 at St. Mary's Catholic Church in Lancaster, New York. My father, Clarence Molinaro, was a New York state trooper. My mother, Helen, along with the entire bridal party, was photographed at a studio in Buffalo.
LORAINE SAIK
RENO, NV

We met at a dance one night in 1948. I was doing the Hucklebuck with a girlfriend, and Tony told his buddies, "Hands off. She's mine." I wasn't interested in getting serious, but after five dates, he kissed me. That was it. It was like the Fourth of July.

ELENA DUDA · LAS VEGAS, NV

HAPPILY STUCK TOGETHER

My dad, Gordon Head, and my mom, Jeannette Holcomb, met at a church gathering in Springboro, Pennsylvania, in 1940. Mom was 18 and thought Dad, at 23, was too old for her. But five years later when Dad returned from serving in World War II, the two were soon dating. While waiting for help after getting his car stuck in the mud, Dad popped the question. They were married on Nov. 14, 1945.

KATHLEEN McDONALD · ERIE, PA

Clothes Make the Man

And a good suit looks as good in the city as it does in the country.

From his buttoned-down vest to the crisp cut of his trousers, my father, Henry Niichel, looked good in a suit—especially when standing in front of a convertible beside a smiling woman.

When Daddy was in his mid-20s, he moved to Chicago, Illinois, where jobs were more plentiful than in his hometown of Granville, Iowa. During his three years there he worked in the textile industry, selecting fabrics from woolen manufacturers to be made into tailored suits.

He was offered a job as a detective on the Chicago police force because he had a talent for remembering people and their mannerisms. He turned the offer down because, my mother said, he very much liked his job in the clothing industry.

In 1933, my father received a letter in Chicago from his younger sister Rose. She was getting married and wanted him home for her wedding.

Having grown up in the area with a population of less than 400, my father knew everyone, including my mother. When she was 15 she told a friend he was the guy she was going to marry.

So when he came back, she asked him to stay. He never did return to Chicago.

In Iowa, Daddy worked as a telephone lineman. Saving their money, my mother and father were engaged for two years before marrying in 1936. Before long they moved from their apartment in Granville to my grandparents' farm northwest of town.

Two days after their first wedding anniversary, Aug. 15, 1937, I was born. Mother said I was her anniversary gift.

When my parents weren't raising oats, corn, pigs, cattle and chickens or caring for their seven children, one of their favorite pastimes was taking drives in the country. As the first child, I got to ride in their roadster, telling my mother, "You ride in the rumble seat, and I'll ride in the front seat by Daddy."

My parents were married for 45 years until my father died in December 1981. Mom died at 93 in November 2007.

ANNETTE NIICHEL PLAGGE · LA PALMA, CA

Up to Date

I met Wes in 1948 when he came to visit his Navy buddy. I was 17 and Wes was 23. When we started dating, I was the envy of all the girls at school. We're still in love and married after all these years.

NORMA WINGERT · NORTH MANCHESTER, IN

CHAPTER 4

....

RETRO
FUN

Smiling with the team, friends, family or
classmates—it doesn't much matter when
you are all having a grand time.

Roadside Refreshment

Every Lyons family vacation began by packing the station wagon with children, coolers and suitcases. We always stopped for lunch on the road—whenever Dad (Frank) spotted a picnic table. Lunch was always the same: bologna sandwich, potato chips and Kool-Aid. This picture taken at Lake Erie, Pennsylvania, in 1968 shows Paul, Judy, Rose (Mother), myself, Tom and Tim.

SUSAN LYONS DIETRICH · MONACA, PA

Teams rode buses to the cities where they played. Here, four members of the 1953 Rockford Peaches say goodbye to family and friends before boarding for the next town.

Dreams Really Do Come True

Determination drove her to play ball
halfway across the country.

W hen my high school softball coach told me at the end of my senior year that she knew the chaperone from a team of professional women baseball players, I knew what I had to do. I drove to the woman's home, about 30 miles away, and played catch with her in her driveway.

That chaperone turned out to be Dottie Green, a former catcher who now worked for the Rockford Peaches.

Apparently I passed the test with flying colors, because about two weeks later I received a contract offering me $225 a month for the 1953 season. Accepting the offer was a no-brainer for me. Playing baseball at a high level was something I'd always dreamed of doing. So in the spring of 1953, when I was 17, I took the train from Boston, Massachusetts, to South Bend, Indiana, where I started spring training with the Peaches.

Dottie met me in Indiana and assigned me a roommate, Dolores "Pickles" Lee from Jersey City, New Jersey. Pickles loved to talk and was never at a loss for words. She also was a heavy sleeper, and more than once we did laps around the track for being late to practice. But we were close friends and remained that way for the next 60 years until her death in 2014.

The best part of my experience was playing with such talented players. The worst part, being notified the league had ended. I was left with only the memory of two of the best years of my life.

SUE PARSONS ZIPAY
ENGLEWOOD, FL

Paid to Play

The All-American Girls Professional Baseball League brought women into the limelight.

T he four seasons I spent in 1951-'54 playing baseball for the Fort Wayne Daisies and the South Bend Blue Sox were the best years—great fun—and I got paid to play. It doesn't get any better than that.

When I was 16, I attended a game in Fort Wayne, Indiana, and tried out for the team the very next day. Then I went back home to Westfield Center, Ohio, and waited to hear from the organization.

In January 1951, I was a senior in high school when I got my invitation to arrive at spring training. I arranged with school to complete a few assignments and send homework to one teacher. Then I left for Alexandria, Virginia, to train. The week I came home, I attended my senior prom, graduated from high school and became a Fort Wayne Daisy.

We played 110 games a season, seven nights a week with double-headers on Sunday. We wore a one-piece dress for a uniform. It was important to the Wrigleys that we looked like ladies. As one player explained, "We were expected to look like Betty Grable and play ball like Joe DiMaggio."

Our lives consisted of day practice, night games and bus trips to the next city where we had a game. Our rivalries were not among our teammates, but with the team we were playing on any given night.

My single claim to fame came one night in 1953 while playing for the South Bend Blue Sox. I was catching a perfect game thrown by superstar Jean Faut against the Kalamazoo Lassies. We never talked about it on the bench, but teammates Betty Wagoner and Jeep Stoll caught the only two balls that made it out of the infield to clinch the game.

In 1952 the Fort Wayne Daisies coach was the great slugger and Hall of Famer Jimmie Foxx. Reviewers thought Jimmy Dugan, the Tom Hanks character in the movie *A League of Their Own*, was a thinly veiled Jimmie Foxx. I played for him and can set the record straight: Jimmie was a true gentleman. We never saw him take a drink, he never missed a game, and we adored him.

LOIS YOUNGEN · EUGENE, OR

After retiring from baseball, Lois Youngen earned a doctorate and became director of physical activity and recreation services at the University of Oregon. She sits on the board of the AAGPBL Players Association.

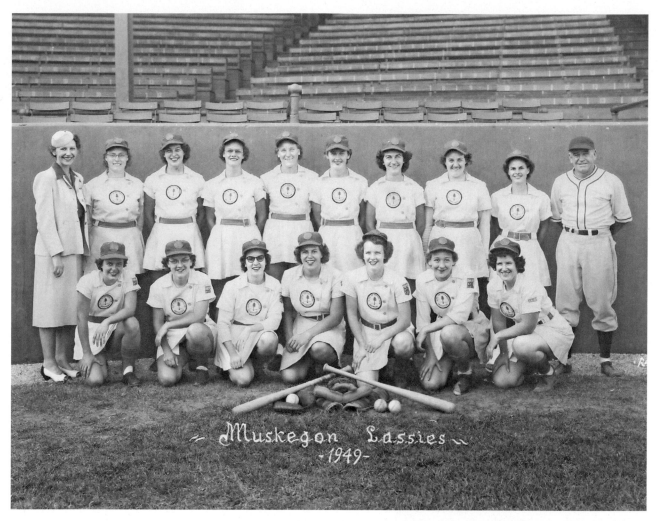

GO, TEAM, GO!
The 15 members of the Muskegon Lassies gathered in 1949 for a photo with chaperone Helen Hannah and manager Carson Bigbee. The team played in the league from 1946 to 1950.
PHOTO COURTESY OF THE HISTORY MUSEUM · SOUTH BEND, IN

BETSY JOCHUM
outfield-first base-pitcher

HARD HITTER
After I read about tryouts in the paper, I went to Chicago from my home in Cincinnati, Ohio, and competed with 400 other girls. I made the cut and was an original team member of the South Bend Blue Sox. And in 1944, I won the batting crown.
BETSY "SOCKUM" JOCHUM
SOUTH BEND, IN

Salty with a Side of Sass

Envisioning her future, she would have played ball for free if asked.

———

Baseball was my life. From the time I was 4 and went to a baseball game with my dad, I wanted to play. I told everyone I was going to be a professional ballplayer when I grew up. I didn't even know if that was possible, but I knew that's what I wanted to do.

Growing up in Orangeville, Pennsylvania, I played all kinds of sports with the boys in the neighborhood. They would knock on our front door and ask my mom if I could come out and play.

I was also a batgirl for the local men's team and dressed in the catcher's gear to warm up the batters.

Then in 1952, Paul Reichart, a friend of the family's, was doing business in Allentown with Charles Schuler, a scout for the All-American Girls Professional Baseball League. Reichart told the scout about me, and I was invited to visit Schuler for a tryout.

My father drove with me to Allentown, where we met

Although her batting average was just over .200, Salty's fielding percentage was .936.

Schuler at a park. After I threw five pitches, Schuler walked back and told my father, "I'm sending her to the Rockford Peaches." My feet didn't touch the ground until I got home and told my mother.

I needed permission from the principal to finish school early, but after that, I was off to South Bend, Indiana, for spring training. My parents came with me, and my dad signed my first contract (I was only 17). They soon realized that for me to succeed, they had to go home. Little did they know that I would never have given up.

My manager was John Rawlings, and there were 18 players on the team. We could fill a stadium because people loved seeing women in dresses play the game. I played right field and catcher. Even though I was never a big hitter, I was known for my defensive skills and my rifle arm.

SARAH JANE "SALTY" SANDS FERGUSON
ORANGEVILLE, PA

1943
The year the All-American Girls Professional Baseball League was founded by Major League Baseball team owner and chewing gum mogul Philip K. Wrigley. The female ballplayers replaced the male teams whittled down during WWII.

....

60
Number of players on the original roster of four teams: the Kenosha Comets and the Racine Belles of Wisconsin; the Rockford Peaches of Illinois; and the South Bend Blue Sox of Indiana.

....

910,000
Peak game attendance, in 1948. Over the years, 10 additional teams were added, all from the Midwest.

....

12
Number of years the league ran, disbanding in 1954.

....

640
Number of women employed as ballplayers during the league's run.

Little did they know that I would never have given up.

Groovy duds were the uniform for, from left, Allie Masood, Jim Bulger, Bob Watkins, Tom McGhee and Monte Maugle.

LOCALLY FAMOUS

SAXTON, A SMALL RURAL TOWN IN the south-central hills of Pennsylvania, was teeming with local bands in the mid-'60s, all sharing the dream of becoming teenage idols while playing guitar, drums and keyboards. I was one of those teens.

For years, I took piano lessons, mainly to please my mother, when I would rather have been playing baseball. But when my love of music took over, I purchased a keyboard and an amplifier to join the craze.

I jammed with some local musicians before forming Ye Loste Souls with four friends. The name denotes our mindset of being lost in the music and wanting to share it with others. The group included Tom McGhee, a self-taught musician rarely seen without his guitar; Monte Maugle, drummer for the high school band; and Jim Bulger and Allie Masood, both of whom had been taking guitar lessons for

years. We practiced in Allie's basement and learned all the songs on the Top 40 charts by the Beatles, Rolling Stones, Animals, Dave Clark Five, Rascals, Beach Boys, Three Dog Night, Grass Roots, Tommy James and the Shondells, and The Byrds.

We debuted at our high school assembly and in no time were performing at local teen dances. Our sound man, Donnie Benner, got us booked in dance halls, gyms and clubs throughout central Pennsylvania. We stayed together for six years until college, the Navy, jobs, marriage and kids changed our priorities.

Thirty years later, the editor of the local newspaper planned a reunion concert of the two most popular local bands of the '60s, Ye Loste Souls and The Outcast Society. We played on Aug. 28, 1998, to a crowd of about 1,000 and raised $2,000 for a local charity. We may not have made it to the big stage, but those memories will last a lifetime.

ROBERT E. WATKINS · SAXTON, PA

IN SYNC

Everyone had a garage band in the 1960s. The Avantis played in Roswell, New Mexico, in 1963 and starred, from left, Salmons on drums, myself, Saturnino "Satie" Chavez and George Szabo. I admit we were pretty bad, but our red-pinstriped Kingston Trio-look shirts made us look cool.

STEVE SCARANO
VISTA, CA

Rock's glory days found, from left, Paul, Doc, Lucky and Wayne wearing gold satin shirts for their gigs.

KNIGHTS IN GOLD SATIN

Starting a rock band in 1966, I recruited my friends Don "Doc" Steele, Eddie "Lucky" D'Giaccomo and Wayne Devine. As The Capps, we played events for our area's top radio stations at the time—WIBG-AM and WFIL-AM. In 1967, we opened for The Soul Survivors and toured with them as they promoted their big hit "Expressway to Your Heart." I still entertain professionally.

PAUL BIG BEAR · ABINGTON, PA

The Showmen, from left, Mike Gutsch, Snuffy Smith, Dave Preston, Bob Lee and Terry Hoeppner.

THEIR BIG BREAK

When our group, Bob Lee & the Showmen, were asked to play at Fournier's Ballroom in Eau Claire, Wisconsin, owners Lou and Carl Fournier had one condition: Come back to play here again when you become famous. The couple never enforced the deal, but the band leveraged that booking to get gigs at other dance clubs and ballrooms. We even became the house band for Shorty's Shack in La Crosse.
DAVE PRESTON · MENOMONIE, WI

WHEN FAME IS FLEETING

Finishing second out of 15 in a Battle of the Bands contest in Modesto, California, in 1967, Maximum Capacity won a 12-string guitar and six hours of recording time. Not bad for a band that practiced at my grandmother's house. The group opened in Modesto for Eric Burdon and the Animals and in San Francisco at the legendary Fillmore for the Chambers Brothers.
CHARLES JAMES MOORE
SILOAM SPRINGS, AR

JUST DO YOUR THING

Formed in 1964, London Fog with the Continentals played high school dances, battles of the bands and nightclubs in the Dayton, Ohio, area. The soul group had its own TV show in '69 called *Do Your Thing* on a local station. National bands were the guests. The band broke up when the draft called. I'm the wife of bass player Danny.

JEAN CONNAUGHTON • DAYTON, OH

London Fog with the Continentals

Band members: Top row from left, Quinn Moorman, Danny Connaughton, John Mortimer, Gary Kaiser, Vince DiSalvo; bottom row, Gary Morman, Loretta Reid and Buddy Kraft.

ROLL WITH IT

SKATING ALONG
My sister Nora LaRiviere was already a very skilled skater when this picture was taken at the West Yarmouth, Massachusetts, rink in 1947.
RITA LOUISE WALLACE · CORTEZ, CO

HOMEMADE BUMPER ⌄

In 1966, I was teaching myself to skate in front of our house in Redondo Beach, California, with a pillow to soften my falls. I was 5 at the time and couldn't understand all the interest from passers-by.

CHERYL BONNER · MIDDLEBURG, FL

COMEBACK KID »

Living in Brooklyn, New York, I skated three times a week until I got married in 1960. I took up the hobby again in the mid-1990s.

BEATRICE HANSEN
BROOKLYN, NY

LIFELONG FUN ⌃

I took up skating in 1941 and competed through the mid-1940s. A number of years ago, I joined a Friday morning skate group at a local rink and kept it up into my late 80s.

GLORIA MOORE · OMAHA, NE

This home ec teacher instructs students as they place pattern pieces on their chosen fabric.

Boys' Pranks Had Her in Stitches

Some jokers and a sweet teacher made it memorable.

Home economics was one of those classes that was mandatory in order to graduate from our high school.

I went to Helix High in La Mesa, California, and waited until my senior year in 1964-'65 to take the dreaded class. Unlike most of the girls I knew, I had never made anything, let alone clothing, and my mother didn't own a sewing machine.

By the time I had to take home ec, the school had made an interesting change in its requirement. Any girl who wanted to could take shop instead of home ec, and any boy could take home ec in place of shop.

Evidently, the entire varsity football team got together that year and decided to take home ec. Most of the boys were in my class, and every day was something different.

Our teacher, Miss Kloos, was very sweet and had a wonderful southern accent. The boys teased her mercilessly. They would hide her keys and pull other harmless pranks. She would blush and, in her smooth drawl, say, "Now, boys!" She had a good sense of humor and never got angry.

Our first class assignment was to make an apron. I was at a loss and couldn't sew a straight seam to save my life. We were allowed to work on our projects at home but, of course, that did me no good. I was relieved when my apron was finished. I think most of the boys' aprons came out better than mine.

A photo appeared in our yearbook of some of the guys wearing their aprons and chef hats. One boy we called Fish found fabric with primary-colored polka dots that looked like the Wonder Bread wrapper.

I don't remember much about the cooking part because it didn't interest me. But I still chuckle when I think about that class and what a memorable senior year I had. The class that I most dreaded is where my favorite memories from high school were made.

JUDI CARROLL · ESCONDIDO, CA

THREADS OF THE PAST

Learning in a classroom environment turned the drudgery of housework into a finished project.

« 1940

Looking Good
Singer's 1940 fashion forecast called for full skirts with lots of pockets: "your clothes will be covered with them." Gray and hot pink was one trendy color combo.

1940 »

Class Project
Attending Cleveland Junior High School in Newark, New Jersey, I received this brochure in home ec class. The Spring Summer 1940 issue of *New Fashions for You and Your Home* from Singer Sewing Machine Co., included patterns, project ideas and a look at fashion and fabrics.
MARGARET BACHA
BOCA RATON, FL

By the 1960s, class enrollment in home ec opened up to boys as well as girls.

Lessons Made to Last

Sewing pointers he picked up in home ec stuck with him longer than the lousy recipes.

—

During my eighth grade year, 1972-'73, my school, Morgantown Junior High in Morgantown, West Virginia, offered a coed approach to wood shop and home economics. All students took units in shop, cooking and sewing.

I hadn't inherited Dad's gift for woodworking so, after an unsuccessful unit of shop, I looked forward to taking home economics.

I was already pretty good at cooking, having learned from my mother and grandmother. Classroom instruction came mostly from a 1947 textbook. I don't know where our teacher, Mrs. Pitcher, got the recipes we used, but they were not good. If she cooked like that at home, her family must have eaten out a lot.

My final unit was sewing. I expected to learn nothing more than how to sew on a button in an emergency.

Instead, Mrs. Smith taught us how to cut out a pattern, use a sewing machine, thread bobbins and more.

Because it was a pilot program, the boys were limited in the projects we could choose. While the girls were making dresses, suits and evening gowns, the boys got to make aprons and athletic shorts.

My best creation was a pair of all-cotton purple shorts that I wore until college, when they finally fell apart. But that class left a lasting impression. I still own a sewing machine. I can hem pants in less than half an hour and patch worn spots so they don't show.

I wonder if they still teach home ec. My younger friends are utterly lost in the kitchen and at a sewing machine. I'm grateful for having learned skills that have benefited me throughout my life.

DAVID L. WASSON
BUCKHANNON, WV

THAT CLASS WAS SEW FUNNY

My sister Patsy and I learned to make dresses when we were 12. We used an old cast-iron treadle machine. When I started home ec in 1964, I watched as the teacher showed how to use a modern sewing machine. Not seeing a treadle or foot pedal, I whispered to the girl next to me, "What's making the machine go?" She paused and said, "Electricity."
KATHRYN AGULAR · WESTPORT, MA

THE DEMISE OF DOMESTIC SCIENCE

The Morrill Act of 1862 established land-grant colleges and universities that boosted enrollment of women and low-income and rural students. The mandated programs focused on research and practical endeavors including domestic science.

....

In 1876, Ellen Swallow Richards, a chemist and instructor at the Massachusetts Institute of Technology—and the first woman to earn a degree from MIT—helped establish the Women's Laboratory, with courses that applied a scientific approach to domestic concerns.

....

Starting in 1899, Richards organized an annual conference of educators in Lake Placid, New York. This group coined the term home economics and in 1908 formed the American Home Economics Association, later renamed the American Association of Family & Consumer Sciences.

....

During the Depression, school funding for home ec programs waned, but where maintained, women learned to cook efficiently and sew and mend clothing.

....

In the era following World War II, new technologies and store-bought conveniences made from-scratch cooking and sewing seem outdated.

....

Today, home ec class offerings have shrunk because of limited resources and the lack of qualified teachers.

SUMMER SCENES

BATHING BEAUTY
This photo of my wife, Barbara, was taken in 1959, the first year of our marriage. We were staying at the Sans Souci Hotel in Miami Beach, Florida. *Sans souci* is French for "carefree," and I think this picture captures that feeling—along with Barbara's beautiful smile.
TOM LARONGA · SEBAGO, ME

« CHEERS TO YOUTH

On most Sundays after Mass, all the guys would meet up for stickball, leapfrog or hide-and-seek. Or we'd hang out in my backyard with Mom. Here we are in 1962 at our house in East Newark: from left, Rose Mary Pagano, Peter Borghesi, Billy Heffern, John Hess and Robert Kreese. I'm in front in the striped shirt.

SAM PAGANO
MORRISTOWN, NJ

BRIGHT MEMORY ⌄

I love this 1958 photo of my brothers Joe and Jeff with our mom relaxing by the public pool. It takes me back. Even though it was more than 60 years ago, the memory is crystal clear. I can practically smell the chlorine in the air.

GREG GROOM · COLUMBUS, OH

Mom (Jerri) and I with my brothers Steve and Rich look like cool cats on a very warm summer day at Six Flags Over Texas in 1966.

TAMARA MORAN-SMITH
TULSA, OK

SUMMER SCENES

ATLANTIC INVASION

In the summer of 1958, the insufferable heat of our hometown of Ridgewood, New Jersey, was suffocating my five siblings and me. So we were overjoyed when Dad announced we were going to Massachusetts to spend two weeks at a cottage in South Wellfleet on Cape Cod. From left: Matthew, 8, Geraldine, 3, Mom Peg, Daniel, 6, Patrick, 10, myself, 11, and Margaret Mary, 4.

MIKE MULHERN
PONTE VEDRA
BEACH, FL

A WHEEL-DEAL CELEBRATION

We celebrated my 8th birthday in 1955 cruising the streets of West Tulsa in the Party Wagon. The driver picked us up, gave us a cold bottle of pop and drove us around the neighborhood. My 5-year-old sister cried the whole way, but we had a good time anyway. I'm the second one from the left.

JEARLD McAFEE
SAND SPRINGS, OK

AEROPLANE VIEW OF CHAIN O'LAKES. WAUPACA. WIS.

A vintage postcard showing part of Wisconsin's Chain o' Lakes region.

Life on Little Chain

With a ring of the bell and a jump off the pier, the season was up and running.

Back in 1942, my grandparents bought property in Waupaca, Wisconsin, in an area known as the Chain o' Lakes. Poppy's 2½ acres were on Lake Orlando on the Little Chain. By the time I was 10, we were going up there every summer.

There were two cottages done in beautiful knotty pine—Big House and Little House—built by my father, uncles and Poppy, with help from some boys in town. My brother Roy and I slept in the living room under two stuffed moose heads. When our cousins came, we were a crowd. People spilled over onto the screened porches, sleeping on World War II-era Army cots. I can still hear the sound of that screen door slamming as I'd run out to play in the yard, where my favorite swing was always waiting for me.

Mornings you could hear doves cooing and at night, the singing of crickets. We had a large bell in the yard and Dad, known as Buddy, would ring it whenever someone arrived. He'd blow a bugle when they left. He was so fun-loving.

The first cutting of the grass after winter had to be done with a sickle. Everyone worked as a team; the women cleaned the cottages as the men tended to the grounds. We kids went swimming in a roped-off area or, once you were a better swimmer, off the pier.

Occasionally you'd hear someone yell, "Don't go down to the lake! Uncle Buddy is taking a bath!"

Sometimes we went to our neighbor's on Beasley Creek, where the water was sparkling clear and barely a foot deep over a sandy bottom. To get from Big Chain to Little Chain you had to go through the creek, pulling your boat behind. Many made the crossing to get to Whispering Pines Park on Marl Lake, where there was a concession stand, museum and gift shop. For a penny we could feed oatmeal to the fish.

Priests from the Jesuit summer home on the Big Chain would row around the lakes and sing. We'd hear them while we barbecued hot dogs and toasted marshmallows.

On special occasions we'd have dinner at a fancy restaurant in town, sometimes staying to see a movie at the Palace or the Rosa. A boat ride would take us to Ding's Dock and the casino, where we saw Ricky Nelson and Louis Armstrong perform.

Mostly, though, we were happy to stay at Poppy's, swimming and fishing. Dad caught a 12-inch bass once; he was so proud of it, he had it mounted.

We sold the cottages in 1961, but Waupaca will definitely be in my heart forever. If you're lucky enough to have a summer cottage on a lake, you're lucky enough.

JEANNETTE CURIA · ALGONQUIN, IL

Swimmers crowd a pool on a hot day at Jones Beach State Park on New York's Long Island around 1960.

Poolside Playbook

Coppertone, Zero bars and that kid
who dunked everyone.

As the weather starts to warm up, my memories always take me back to the public swimming pool in our neighborhood. That was the center of the universe for the kids of the Lindenwald district of Hamilton in the summers of the 1960s.

After paying 25 cents, we'd toss our belongings in a metal basket and turn it in at the desk for a pin with a number that we attached to our swimsuits. Our folks were comfortable turning us loose there unaccompanied because the man in charge, the aptly named Mr. Sharp, ran a tight ship: No running; no horseplay (whatever that was); no food or drink in the pool area. Any rowdy type, usually a boy, who didn't follow the rules had to sit out on what Mr. Sharp called "the penalty bench."

One particularly pesky kid, whom I'll call Charlie to protect the innocent, would dunk the girls or splash them when they walked by, and always cut into line at the concession stand. A good day at the pool was when Charlie spent the better part of it on the penalty bench.

Pool breaks—when the pool was emptied of kids so the adults could swim in peace—were touted as a chance for the kids to rest. But I think it was a conspiracy to increase profits at the concession stand because that's where we headed. Our biggest decision of the day was whether to get a pop and popcorn or a pop and a frozen Zero bar. When the whistle blew again, it was back into the water.

Not so for the older girls, of course. They all carried train cases—those small, boxy pieces of luggage—and would set out their baby oil and Coppertone and other beauty aids on their neatly arranged towels, ready for an afternoon of gossip and tanning.

Those girls didn't get in the pool very often; they didn't want to muss their hair, I guess. Perhaps they had good reason: All the teenage boys who were too cool for the pool would hang around the fence, ogling the girls in their cute swimsuits.

The public pools in our town are all gone now. I know we can't go back, but such a big chunk of our growing up was spent at those pools that the closings make me sad. Splashing around, being with friends, even having to deal with the Charlies of the world—life at a public pool was good.

I wonder whatever happened to Charlie? If there's any justice in this world, he had to raise five sons who cannonballed him every chance they got.

MARYSUE WRIGHT · HAMILTON, OH

No Station Wagon Needed

Bike riding was a favorite pastime for my family. This picture of my
siblings Paul, Peter and Carol was taken outside our family home
in Garden City, Michigan, in 1967. Peter and Carol are still
as close as they are here.

SALLY OLSON · HARBOR SPRINGS, MI

CHAPTER 5

AT
WORK

Enjoy accounts of those who rolled up
their sleeves and got the job done, and of
others who found the right career path.

Honeywell Shine

After high school, I worked at Honeywell in Minneapolis,
where every month they'd put out a newsletter with a calendar
girl. The day this picture was taken in 1961 was cold and drizzly.
The color must have been enhanced because my black swimsuit
came out almost purple and my hair, though red, wasn't quite
that red. The company printed out several copies for me to sign.
I have very fond memories of working for Honeywell.

JOHNNIE MARTIN CHAPLINSKI · MIDDLE RIVER, MN

Siblings and business partners, John and Stella share time with the boys.

Corner Fix-It Shop
Found Its Focus

Dad made repairs while his sister kept the books.

——

M y father, John Wentzel, and his sister, Stella, were born in Newton, Kansas. They both joined the armed services during World War II. Dad was in the Army and Stella, in the Women's Army Corps. There she met Louise Riederer, from New Rochelle, New York. Stella introduced her brother to her friend and fellow WAC, and John and Louise soon married.

After the war in 1946, my parents, along with Aunt Stella, settled in San Francisco and started their own business, Aladdin Radio Repair. They originally ran the business out of a rented storefront on Seventh Avenue in the city, but in

1951 they moved to a building they had purchased at 17th and Irving, about 10 blocks west of the original store. By that time televisions were becoming quite popular, and Dad added TV repair to his repertoire.

Dad did the repairs and made service calls while Stella handled customers, accounting and any related paperwork. The two-story building they bought for the business included a two-bedroom, one-bath flat upstairs, keeping the business conveniently close to home.

Mom initially worked at a liquor store downtown but quit when she became pregnant with me. I was born in 1949, followed by my brother, James, in

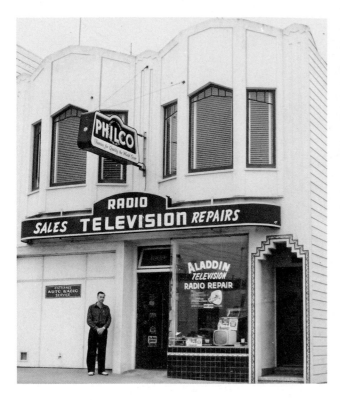

Clockwise from left: John outside the current store; Bob and Jim show off their wheels as parents John and Louise smile proudly in 1954; Stella in 1946 stands outside their first location; John still spends a few hours a day in his shop.

1951. When James and I were preteens, Mom started working for a friend at his jewelry shop.

Stella passed away in December 1983, leaving my parents to run the business by themselves. Meanwhile televisions were becoming more advanced, with more and more electronics. They were also more difficult to work on, so Dad phased them out and focused on repairing radios, including those in cars.

When my mother died in April 2010, Dad scaled back the business to more of a hobby, focusing exclusively on antique radio repair and restoration. Now in his 90s, he still spends a few hours a day in his shop, fixing a radio, tutoring a younger future repairman, or visiting with friends and giving helpful advice.

His shop remains much as it has been for many years—long shelves lined with antique radios and related electronic odds and ends. His workbench, which is still in daily use, is crammed with vintage diagnostic equipment. There's a showroom stocked with restored vintage floor- and table-model radios and phonographs, and a big picture window, filled with all sorts of collectibles and pictures, facing the sidewalk where passersby stop to look.

Neither James nor I pursued the radio repair trade. I am a retired auto mechanic and James is a retired machinist, living in San Francisco a few blocks from where we were raised.

ROBERT WENTZEL · SEBASTOPOL, CA

Carol, 16, took off her coat to play ball at a fall picnic, above, in 1943. She lived on her parents' farm in Angola, Indiana, opposite.

Standing Up for Working Women

Don't believe everything you read in the papers.

W hile World War II raged overseas and eligible bachelors joined the military ranks, young women like my mother, Carol Sheets, stayed home, dressed in slacks and went to work in the factories. My mother found a good job at the Magnavox plant in Fort Wayne, Indiana.

After working at Magnavox for a time, my mom sent a letter to the editor of the local newspaper. She had read something that didn't quite sit right with her. It's an early glimpse of her true grit:

To the Editor,

I read with amusement, then with resentment, "Servicemen Want Homemaking Girls."

I think it is rather discouraging to the girls of the United States—the many girls that are working hard in a factory all day—to come home and discover that the boys don't like our type of girls, and to read about all the boys that are getting married to the girls who are overseas where they have been fighting.

After all, we didn't ask for this war. Neither did anyone else for that matter.

But we were forced to do something about it, and so we donned our slacks and went to work to help do our part in taking care of Hitler and Tojo and their mugs.

Well, it was our patriotic duty to do this. Maybe we don't like to. Perhaps we'd like to run a home. Right now almost everyone's plans are mixed up a little. But I think the girls in those other countries are carrying it a bit too far when they criticize us. First they didn't like our knees because we wore our dresses too short and so forth. And now it seems that the American boys want girls to be the homemaking type.

Now I ask you, girls, just what are we waiting for if it isn't for the boys to come home to have homes? Maybe someday those boys will realize that the cooking American girls do isn't so bad after all.

How about it, girls? What do you say? Don't you think that they're going a bit too far????

Just another United States girl,

C.S.

The war ended in 1945 and my mother left Magnavox after a few years. In 1948 she met my father, Bob Scarlett, and they were married in 1949. They had four children, three girls and a boy.

Almost a decade later, from 1957 to 1976, my mom worked at Wagner Industries, a manufacturer of automobile parts in Reading, Michigan. When the company hired 18-year-old men at a starting wage much higher than that of female employees who had been there for years, the union hired an attorney.

They reached a settlement and Wagner compensated the women, paying the back wages that were due. My mother was proud of the difference she'd made with that historic process and decision.

ELLYN SCARLETT · ELKHART, IN

Wensley Pattern Works in Lynn, Massachusetts, made patterns for nearby General Electric and other customers. Photos of the shop were taken in 1925.

Intricate Work on the Shop Floor

When manufacturing was an art and a science.

A t the Wensley Pattern Works in Lynn, Massachusetts, in the early 1920s, workers dressed neatly, often wearing white shirts, ties and suspenders. The workshop was organized with overhead belt drives and visible, rather haphazard electrical wiring.

Everyone had access to the tools needed for the work. Dozens of parallel clamps hung from walls or from center posts. The sprinkler system was overhead, and telephone bells were situated on the walls or on overhead beams. Prized Emmert vises were fitted to most of the workbenches, which had tool chests underneath them.

Years later, I owned and operated the shop from 1970 to 1976 and employed four people. We made patterns for aluminum, brass and cast-iron castings. One of the patterns was for an 8-foot-diameter door that fit a tubular kiln. When a fire destroyed the building, I was forced to close the shop.

But I still enjoy reminiscing about the old-time patternmakers who fabricated complicated designs and models aided only by a few antiquated machines and their own skilled handcraftsmanship. It's like night and day compared to today's shops.

Now, computer-aided design and numerous other manufacturing processes such as die casting, injection molding, thermoforming and 3D printing have replaced the pattern shops of bygone days.

At 92, I believe that those old-time patternmakers should be remembered and held in high esteem for their wonderful craftsmanship and the inestimable contributions they made to everyday life.

JOSEPH F. SADLOW · NORTH READING, MA

At his workbench, James Clark employs an Emmert vise for patternmakers.

With great tunes and simple fare, the restaurant was a hit with teens.

Hog Heaven

A barbecue sandwich, a Coke and a date
were all you needed on a Friday night.

———

Great memories return whenever I think of the years from 1956 to 1967. They were the best 12 years any child could have had. All my school friends loved getting off the bus at my house because my parents owned and operated the Old Hickory Barbeque Restaurant. Every day, Mama and Daddy would build a hickory wood fire and smoke fresh hams. You could smell that good southern aroma as soon as you pulled under the awning for service.

Back then, most of the local teenagers came to our restaurant to get barbecue sandwiches or cheeseburgers, fries, and an ice-cold Coca-Cola. While eating they would play the hit songs of the '50s and '60s on the jukebox.

On Friday nights after the high school ball games, our restaurant was packed. Many young couples started dating and were married after meeting at our diner. I know. I did. And five of my best friends did the same thing.

PAT TURNER · LAWRENCEVILLE, GA

On the edge of Wellsville, New York, our favorite diner stayed open late. The menu item for people who had been out on the town was Graveyard Stew, a fried egg on toast served in a bowl of hot creamy milk. It tasted better than it sounds.

KEITH FOLTS · FILLMORE, NY

Pat's parents ran the restaurant for more than 10 years and even opened a second one.

SHORT-ORDER SHORTHAND

Diner slang let the cook know what to burn and what to put a hat on.

BREAKFAST

Burn the British ....English muffin, toasted
Sinkers and suds ....Doughnuts and coffee
Wreck 'em .... Scrambled eggs

LUNCH

Bossy in a bowl .... Beef stew
Burn one, clean up the kitchen .... Hamburger
First lady...Spare ribs
Radio.. Tuna
Whiskey...Rye bread

CONDIMENTS

Axle grease .... Butter
Paint it red..With ketchup
Sand ....Sugar
Sea dust...Salt
Twins ....Salt and pepper
Warts ....Olives
Yellow paint.. Mustard

SPECIAL ORDERS

High and dry...Served plain
In the alley .... Served on the side
Keep off the grass ....Hold the lettuce
On the hoof...........................Meat cooked rare
On wheels.. To go
Put a hat on it ....Add ice cream

LIBATIONS

Baby juice..Milk
Shake one in the hay ....Strawberry milkshake
Squeeze one ....Orange juice

DESSERT

Eve with a lid on ....Apple pie
Fish eyes..Tapioca pudding
Houseboat...Banana split
Nervous pudding..Jell-O

Hopetown visitors could watch actors re-create exciting scenes like this one on the street outside a hotel.

Everyone Played Their Part

At Bob Hope's movie ranch, work was part of the show.

The summer of 1965, I was 17 and eager to earn enough money to get my own place when I turned 18. So I got a job at Hopetown, Bob Hope's movie ranch in Simi Valley, California. Hope had just purchased the almost 1,900-acre amusement park, originally called Corriganville Movie Ranch.

The ranch was a Western-themed tourist attraction open on weekends in the summer. Silvertown was one of the movie sets, with a jail, restaurant, saloon and various shops for customers to buy snacks and souvenirs. Actors dressed in costumes and staged scenes from actual movies such as *Gunfight at the O.K. Corral*.

The ranch had additional sets and locations used for shooting films including *Fort Apache*, as well as caves, miles of trails and even the Robin Hood Lake and Robin Hood Forest. According to its previous owner, more than 3,000 movies and TV shows had been filmed at Corriganville.

While there, I worked in several of the shops in Silvertown. I met a movie or TV star almost every weekend—including Doug McClure, Johnny Cash, Dan Blocker, George Montgomery and others.

One of the set actors, Bill "Willy" Willingham, took a special liking to me and watched over me the whole time I worked at the ranch. He had a jovial personality and had been a character actor

HOTEL: WWW.CORRIGANVILLE.NET

in lots of old Westerns. Willy introduced me to the entire cast and crew, including the stable master, Gary, who took care of the ranch horses and the stagecoach, giving guests rides and riding lessons.

Gary was tall, dark, handsome and polite. I knew that I was in trouble when our eyes met. He reached out and kissed my hand, and I almost fainted right there. Whenever I worked, I found myself waiting for Gary to walk by, tip his cowboy hat and say hello. My heart would fall into my stomach and gurgle around.

Then one day he stopped and asked me if I would like a stagecoach tour of the ranch after work. I told him yes before he had a chance to change his mind. Gary later taught me how to mount, dismount and ride a horse. After that, I preferred horseback riding to sitting on the hard seat of the stagecoach any day.

One hot day, the ranch manager brought Bob Hope into the shop where I was working. Hope wanted a snow cone and some popcorn, so I made him both. He took the popcorn, looked around and said, "Mary, this place is too clean. It should have some popcorn on the floor." Then he proceeded to throw popcorn at me. We all laughed out loud. Hope was very easygoing and fun to be around.

The second time I ran into Hope on the ranch, he called me by name. His daughter Linda came out to the ranch a couple of times that summer and held horse races after hours with the cowboys. I'm not sure if they let her win, but I know she was quite a horsewoman.

Often at the end of the day after the horses were put away, we would meet cast members at the lake and go swimming. This was also where Johnny Weissmuller of Tarzan fame filmed the *Jungle Jim* TV series. We would stand on a huge rock, hold on to the ropes that Weissmuller used, swing over the lake and drop in.

Hope used the property as a movie ranch for only one year before all movie production stopped. When the ranch closed, Gary took a job in another state and we lost contact.

Now, when I think back about Hopetown, my memories are of the cast and crew, cowboys, my crush on Gary, horseback riding, and meeting Bob Hope and other celebrities. But, most of all, I remember how fortunate I was to get paid for having fun.

MARY ELIZABETH SCHAEFER
STIRLING CITY, CA

A cast picture shows Mary—in the front row with white tennis shoes—standing next to performer Bill "Willy" Willingham in white pants.

Midwest Marilyn

A model publicized movies in true Hollywood style.

——

When I was in my 20s, I had an unusual job promoting movies as a pretend-starlet. It was during a time in the late '50s and early '60s when studios were pouring a lot of money into publicity to compete with TV.

Films were publicized one theater at a time, with grand openings and live models in costumes that matched what was on the big screen. Looking back, I realize I was very lucky to have been in the right place at the right time. Yet, I stumbled onto this path only after an early setback out of high school.

I was about to graduate in my hometown of Appleton, Wisconsin, and thought that I'd be continuing my education my way; I'd taken all college-prep classes and hoped to pursue the arts, especially theater, and then become an actress.

But my mother had other plans for me. She said I had to be a nurse.

Back then, in the mid-1950s, a young woman was expected to become a nurse or a teacher. I didn't want to be either one.

So, disappointed but determined to do something different, I enrolled at Patricia Stevens, a modeling and finishing school in

Diane (with flag) and her sister Susan arrive at a Milwaukee, Wisconsin, movie theater to promote the opening of *Some Like It Hot* in 1959. Diane also did general modeling (far left).

Milwaukee, Wisconsin, with the idea that by the end of my studies I'd be "finished"—polished enough to work for an airline as a flight attendant.

It was a hectic time because I was working as a telephone operator in Appleton. I'd work until 5 p.m., run to the train depot, hop on the express to make a two-hour class in Milwaukee and then ride the milk train home. Sometimes I'd have to go directly to the telephone company for a night shift.

I would've kept this up for months, most likely until I collapsed from exhaustion. But then something unexpected happened: An instructor at the modeling school suggested that I enter the Miss Milwaukee beauty competition.

I was sure I didn't stand a chance because I had no talent I could perform. My mother brushed aside my worries.

"You want to be an actress," she told me. "Why don't you do a dramatic reading?"

So I did. And I won.

That was in 1957. Soon I was making special appearances as Miss Milwaukee. It felt as if I was constantly on call to do a car show here or a store opening there. I never turned down anything. One day a modeling agency called with a special job: It wanted me to tour as a starlet. I wasn't exactly sure what that involved because I wasn't a working actress, but I was intrigued.

Taking it meant I'd have to quit my job at the phone company, drop out of Patricia Stevens and move away from home.

My parents were very upset. They considered Milwaukee to be this big, scary city, which it wasn't, of course.

Mom and Dad were florists and busy with their business. As the oldest child, I handled a lot of the work at home—all the cooking and cleaning, landscaping and gardening, and looking after my

I did postcards for Wisconsin Dells tourism and print ads for Harley-Davidson.

Diane handed out fake wanted posters to folks to publicize the Bob Hope comedy *Alias Jesse James,* which was playing at the Palace Theater in Milwaukee in the summer of 1959.

two younger sisters. My family really didn't want me to leave.

It was a tough decision, but finally a friend sat me down and told me in no uncertain terms that I had to cut the umbilical cord.

So at 21, instead of continuing at Patricia Stevens or becoming a flight attendant, I started working as a model and doing promo spots on the radio and TV, pretending to be a starlet.

The announcer or interviewer would introduce me by saying, "This is Diane Hatch, a starlet who's got a movie coming out."

It really sounds crazy now, but that's just how promotion was done in those days. I was supposed to say that I'd graduated from the Lee Strasberg acting school in New York and that I lived in Chicago and had all these brothers. It was really very silly.

It could also be challenging if the very person interviewing me guessed the truth and tried to trip me up. And it baffled people in the floral industry in Wisconsin, all of whom knew my family—and knew I wasn't a starlet.

The modeling agency probably should've had me use a fake name, but I guess no one thought of it.

To be honest, except for *Some Like It Hot,* I never saw any of the movies I promoted. I think

some of them were pretty forgettable—they needed the extra publicity!

The promotional photos were taken prior to the film's opening, before there were any customers. Sometimes passers-by would stop to talk or shake my hand.

I was doing all kinds of neat things. A car dealership flew me to Copper Harbor, Michigan, for a week's photo shoot. I did postcards for Wisconsin Dells tourism and print ads for Harley-Davidson. I jumped out of big Christmas packages. At a Piggly Wiggly supermarket opening, I had to stand on the roof and reach for the pig.

I didn't model or tour very long, though; I found it lonely, especially if I had to travel to places where I didn't know anyone.

Much later I found my true passion as a jazz radio host, which I did for almost 20 years. I've been a fan of jazz all of my life—I still have an autographed program from a Louis Armstrong concert I attended back in high school.

But I loved my time as a model because you never knew what you were going to do, who you were going to be or what you were going to wear. It was a lot of fun.

DIANE HATCH LOREN · EAST TROY, WI

THE WORKER'S PEN

For those who preferred the elegance of pen to paper over a clunky typewriter.

1963 »

Quite the Gift

Giving one of the world's most wanted pens to someone was definitely a kind gesture. The Parker 45 Insignia option was "a very distinctive present for V.I.P.'s and people you just happen to like immensely." It was 12K gold filled at $15.

« 1953

Drinks the Ink

This ad touts Sheaffer's Snorkel Pen and "How smoothly it glides your thoughts on paper." A nice pen for the '50s working man or woman, its drinking ink action was a convenience over dunking.

Small Screen, Big Dream

Her inspiration came from TV, but the work was all her own.

When I was growing up in Southern California, I'd watch *Emergency!* every Saturday night. I loved that show. And I decided that one day I wanted to be a paramedic.

But in the 10th grade my guidance counselor made it very clear that I needed to squash that dream. First, I was a girl—and fire departments did not hire girls, the counselor said. Second, even if they did take girls, I was 5-foot-2 and too short to be a paramedic.

I was devastated. I graduated from high school in 1980 and went to college to study business. Which I hated.

Fast-forward 35 years. I'd been a stay-at-home mother since our first child was born in 1986. I was reading an article in our local newspaper that said the community was looking for applicants for the ambulance service. I decided to go for it.

At 52 years of age I was accepted. I was certified as an EMT and graduated from paramedic school. Soon after I got my first job as a paramedic.

I'm having the time of my life. It took more than 40 years, but I'm finally working my dream

Paramedics Kevin Tighe and Randolph Mantooth were Lynne's heroes as a teenager.

job, first imagined when I was a teenager watching my favorite show.

I am living proof that you should never give up on your dreams, no matter what others may say. It's never too late.

LYNNE ELSTON · WINDOM, MN

My grandfather William G. Winter owned Saratoga Cab Co. in our hometown in Wisconsin. This picture of him with my father, John, and their dog Rex was taken in the fall of 1937.

JON WINTER · SUPERIOR, WI

THE OTHER WORKHORSE

GREEN PAL »
A farmer's best friend is a good tractor. Case in point, this is a photo of my father raking hay with one of his trusty John Deeres.
ERNEST WILSON

« STILL GOING STRONG AS EVER
I got this tractor in 1948 when I graduated from high school and decided to become a full-time farmer. My parents bought the tractor and some equipment for me in lieu of a college education. The old machine has done a massive amount of work and gone through many mechanical repairs and changes. It is now dedicated to snow removal and debris cleanup, and I use a newer, larger one for fieldwork and heavier tasks. That's me sitting on the tractor then and now.
GEORGE LANCE
ETTERS, PA

Jeff's dad, Dwain, competed with his John Deere. Jeff mowed the lawn with his.

It Had a Lot of Pull

Practical and powerful, tractors were stars in the field and at the fairgrounds.

Most people in our hometown of Bellville, Ohio, know my dad, Dwain Swank, as a John Deere man who loves two-cylinder tractors from the late 1950s. He collects and shows his vintage machines at fairs around the state. He also got his start in the sport of tractor pulling using his Uncle Freeman's John Deere.

Tractor pulling tests both a tractor's strength and a driver's skill. Back in the 1950s and '60s, the contests used step-on sleds and, later, weight exchangers. My dad first competed with John Deeres and then with a modified Farmall at the state and national level.

My folks started taking me to events in the late 1960s. When we went, my mom, Connie, was always too nervous to watch my dad compete, so she had me describe what was happening, grooming me for my current role as a professional tractor-pull announcer.

JEFF SWANK · BELLVILLE, OH

Tractor pulling tests both a tractor's strength and a driver's skill.

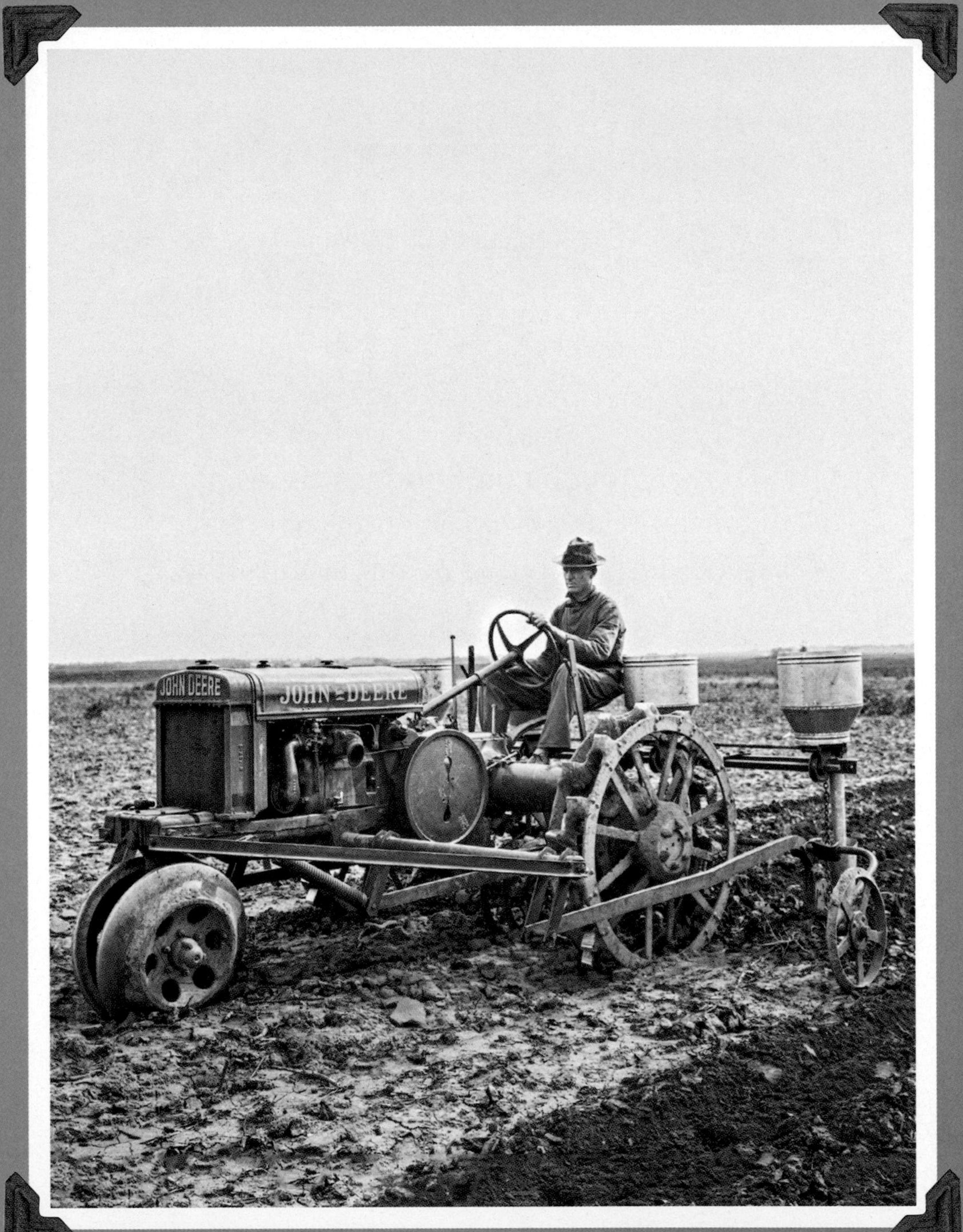

RIGHT: JOHN DEERE & CO.

Making Progress

When John Deere & Co. entered the tractor business in 1918, it knew tractors would revolutionize farming. The company's Model GP, pictured here, was manufactured from 1928 to 1935 and marketed as a general purpose machine.

CHAPTER 6

·····························

OUR
HEROES

Braving tough conditions in times of
uncertainty and despair, those who have
served deserve our love and admiration.

RIGHT: NH 80-G-K-4513 NAVAL HISTORY & HERITAGE COMMAND,
WASHINGTON, DC/US NATIONAL ARCHIVES

At Ease

The crew of the USS *Missouri* enjoys an open-air concert in fair weather
during the ship's shakedown, or testing period, in the summer of 1944.
Music in the armed forces provided a moral boost.

Donald Bloomer's unexpected appearance in a WWII newsreel—on the far right in this still—shocked his brother Gerard, who was serving stateside. At the top of the opposite page are Gerard (left) and Donald's military portraits from 1941.

One Look Was Enough

Spotting his brother in a report about the war in the Pacific inspired joy and renewed fears for his safety.

My father, Gerard, and his big brother Donald enlisted in the Army in early 1941. Gerard joined the engineers and Donald the infantry. Both expected to do a year of service, then get back to their lives, believing, as many did then, that America would never enter World War II.

But a week after the attack on Pearl Harbor, Donald's unit, New York's 27th Infantry Division, was sent to Southern California to guard the West Coast from a possible land attack. The following March, the 27th was deployed to the Pacific to fight on a string of Japanese-held islands that included Guadalcanal, Eniwetok, Saipan, Iwo Jima and Okinawa.

My father was stationed stateside as an explosives expert at Fort Belvoir in Virginia. In early 1945, he was transferred to Augusta, Georgia, for work as a demolition instructor.

One night in April of that year, as he settled in to watch a movie in the Army post theater, my father suddenly shouted in surprise as he looked up at the screen. "Donald!"

He had just recognized his brother in a line of soldiers marching in an MGM newsreel about the 27th Infantry landing on the shores of Okinawa

on April 9, 1945. He watched in amazement as Donald came closer, getting bigger as he neared the camera, then look up, as if directly at my father, before disappearing off screen. It was the next best thing to seeing his brother in person. He immediately asked for a print of that section of film.

Back at his bunk, my father laid the newsreel picture next to all the pictures Donald had taken of the Pacific theater battles in which he'd fought. Dad's buddies, many of whom had not seen actual combat, stood by respectfully, stunned at the brutality of the images. Tears welled in my father's eyes as he thought of what his big brother had been through.

He wrote Donald that night: "For me to sit in a theater and see my big brother walking right towards me, looking right at me…I'll never be able to express in mere words the sensation…"

Donald would survive four major Pacific campaigns—Makin in November 1943, Eniwetok in February 1944, Saipan in June 1944 and Okinawa in April 1945—and receive the Bronze Star for combat action on Saipan.

He was discharged in January 1946 and returned to New York, where he worked as a road sign painter for the state and later for the New York City Water Department.

Donald almost never spoke of the horrors of his war experience. Before he died, however, he told my father that his letters during the war had given him hope and somehow eased the daily terrors of battle. Those letters were the greatest gift my father ever gave his big brother.

MICHAEL BLOOMER · GAINSVILLE, VA

MISSION: NORMANDY

First Lt. LeRoy Blattner, second row far right, poses with other members of his bomber crew on Aug. 2, 1944. The next day, their B-26 Marauder crashed outside the village of Sceaux sur Huisne, France. LeRoy was my brother. I was at the ceremony in 2014 when the community dedicated a memorial to the men. Below their names, the inscription translates as "They died for our freedom."

CHARLOTTE BECKER · HAYS, KS

'Capt. Stewart Was All GI'

The star of *Mr. Smith Goes to Washington* and other films
was more than a Hollywood hero to his WWII squadron.

———

During World War II, I was an armorer with the 445th bomb group, Eighth Air Force, stationed in Tibenham, England. I was responsible for loading the bomb bays and gun turrets of B-24s. One of the planes I was assigned to was *Nine Yanks and a Jerk* under the command of Jimmy Stewart, the movie star who'd put his career on hold to enlist when war broke out.

You wouldn't know an Academy Award winner was in our midst: Capt. Stewart was all GI. He didn't fly easy missions. The men he commanded had a lot of respect for him.

One day, 40 bombers left Tibenham bound for their target, a German supply depot in France. What the pilots didn't know was that their promised return escort of P-51 fighters had mistakenly aligned with a group of B-17s. As the unprotected B-24s headed back, they encountered a wave of German fighters that shot down 27 planes. *Nine Yanks and a Jerk* survived but reached base with a huge hole behind the pilot's seat. I ran to the cockpit. "Sir, are you all right?"

The radio operator was dead and another crew member badly injured. Still seated at his controls, Stewart replied, "Corporal, we got the

LEFT: AP/SHUTTERSTOCK

Stewart had joined our bomb squadron in 1943 as operations officer.

Chuck Larsen was responsible for arming James Stewart's B-24 bomber in World War II. Opposite, the movie legend discusses a mission with his flight crew.

stuffing kicked out of us today!" (Except he didn't say stuffing.)

Stewart had joined our bomb squadron in 1943 as operations officer. We were introduced to the famous captain, then 35, during training near Sioux City, Iowa. After one briefing, Stewart asked us if we had any questions. I put up my hand.

"May I have a Class A pass with your signature on it?"

The actor smiled and said he thought "that could be arranged." We all got one. Unfortunately, when we were leaving for England, the clerk called the passes in—all 400.

My most vivid experience of the war began on June 5, 1944. We'd readied the planes before heading off to chow and some much-needed rest. Suddenly a loudspeaker blasted, "All personnel report to the line for a 2 a.m. mission." So back we went to the airstrip. Each flight crew had only five members per plane, half the normal size. When I asked what was going on, someone said, "We're making history today!"

"You guys make history every day," I told him.

But that day proved to be special. We readied six more planes for a 4 a.m. takeoff, and then another six for a 6 a.m. takeoff. We kept this up for 72 hours straight. D-Day had begun.

CHARLES "CHUCK" LARSEN
WHITE BEAR LAKE, MN

TWO GENERATIONS SERVING TOGETHER

DURING WWII MY FATHER, NEVIL MARTIN, and his brother Roland served in the South Pacific with the all-black infantry unit known as the Harlem Hellfighters. My cousin William "Willie" Martin also was in the Pacific theater at the time with the United States Naval Construction Battalion, more commonly known as the Seabees.

My parents had been married for five years at the time of the attack on Pearl Harbor; I was only 2 when my father went to war. My father was the oldest of the boys in his family, and Roland was the next oldest son. Willie's father, their brother, had passed away some years earlier.

In this picture, both brothers would have been in their mid- to late-20s. Willie was a baby by comparison—he was probably only in his late teens.

CLAUDETTE HOWARD · SCHENECTADY, NY

Nevil Martin, right, and his brother Roland, left, stand with their nephew William shortly after the end of WWII. All three of the men were veterans of the Pacific theater.

Sailing a Peacetime Wave

Seaman recalls the joyous moments immediately after the war ends.

S hortly after the Japanese unofficially surrendered in August 1945, ending World War II, I was a 21-year-old sailor on liberty in Honolulu, Hawaii. We had been at sea for over a year, so to arrive in Hawaii, where the people greeted us warmly, just as the war was ending, was an extraordinary feeling.

We went sightseeing and enjoyed the jubilant atmosphere. Street photographers snapped pictures to document the occasion. Excited children ran along with us, eager to be a part of the celebration.

When America entered the war in 1941, I was 17 and living with my family on a Missouri farm. At that time, the government deferred farmers from active duty to aid the war effort at home. By 1944, however, with the war at its peak, Uncle Sam notified us that one of the Smith sons must report for duty. As the oldest, I felt obliged to serve and chose the Navy. I left my young wife and reported for basic training in Farragut, Idaho, before shipping out on the USS *Latimer* for the Pacific.

The *Latimer* carried troops to and from combat areas. As carpenter's mate, I maintained the mahogany boats that took troops and supplies from ship to shore. Transporting was solemn and silent; we were not allowed to befriend the combat troops. Once, as I watched them being lowered to the boats, I thought the soldiers looked like mere babes—until I realized I was the same age.

Our ship was in the Battle of Luzon in the Philippines and the invasion of Okinawa. After transporting troops and equipment off Okinawa's Hagushi beaches on April 3, 1945, we headed out to sea. At dawn the next day, the Japanese launched an aerial attack that we repelled.

We had a few other close calls, including some attacks by kamikazes—one crashed

Elliott joined in the excitement in Honolulu, Hawaii, when the city learned WWII was coming to an end in August 1945.

within 100 yards of our ship. The planes flew so close that sometimes we could see the faces of the pilots themselves. I was too young to know to be scared; when the alarm sounded, we rushed to our stations and started firing. It truly felt unreal.

That August, we left Honolulu for San Francisco, California. We heard of the official Japanese surrender over the ship's PA system right as we passed under the Golden Gate Bridge. I will never forget that moment.

ELLIOTT M. SMITH · JASPER, AR

George R. Hill Jr., above, showed up in a collection of reproduction military-issue photos of Army tanks—he's standing third from the right.

A Cocked Helmet in Wartime

Son uncovers a piece of Dad's history
in an unlikely flea market find.

My dad, George Robert Hill Jr., fibbed about his age and joined the Army when he was 17, in November 1942. During World War II, he saw action all over Europe, including the Ardennes offensive, commonly called the Battle of the Bulge.

In April 1945, his division liberated the Buchenwald concentration camp, an event Dad was especially proud to have participated in. He was honorably discharged in January 1946.

Dad was in the tank corps and had been part of the crew of an open-top tank fitted with a 105 mm Howitzer gun. He rarely discussed the battles he fought in, the medals he won or the buddies he lost on the battlefield, but occasionally he would talk about the big fighting machine he served on. So I had some idea what it looked like.

Fast forward to January 2013. My wife, Terry, and I were at the Kansas Coliseum flea market north of Wichita. Normally Dad would have joined us—he was always on the lookout for John Wayne or movie-cowboy memorabilia—but he was sick that day. At a booth I saw an envelope labeled "Official Photographs U.S. Army Tanks," and one photo appeared to be very similar to the open-top tank Dad had served on in the war.

Printed on the photo was "105-mm Gun, mounted on a medium tank chassis." After calling my father, who confirmed that was the gun his tank used, I bought the set and sent Dad a copy of the picture.

A few days later, he called. "You must not have looked very closely at that photo," he told me. "Because I'm in it!"

I took a good look this time and, sure enough, there was my father standing in the middle of the group of men, his helmet cocked a little to one side. Dad always wore his helmet that way, which was how he was sure it was him.

I'm still amazed that I just happened to stumble upon something so small yet so significant to our family history amid the thousands of items at that monthly flea market sale. Dad passed away in 2015. The photo of him serving his country will remain a cherished Hill artifact for years to come.

ROGER HILL · WICHITA, KS

WASPs Frances Green, Margaret "Peg" Kirchner, Ann Waldner and Blanche Osborn in front of their B-17, *Pistol Packin' Mama*, in 1944. Though an admirer of the World War II Army Air Forces, Adrian, below right, chose the Army during the Korean War.

War Birds Overhead

Women were their own force in the air.

Military aircraft often flew over our community in Mount Sterling, Kentucky, when I was kid in the early 1940s. They were en route from the factories to the fighting overseas. Throughout World War II, it wasn't unusual for us to look up and see 10 or 15 bombers and several fighter planes, all heading east.

One afternoon in 1944, when I was 12, all of us in the two-room Sideview school heard a distant rumbling that soon grew so loud none of us could concentrate. We ran to the windows and saw four heavy bombers flying about 200 feet off the ground, very close to our school. We'd never seen planes flying that low.

I was too young to serve in World War II, but I did serve a tour of duty in Korea when I was older. A few years after my military service, I was elected to the state General Assembly, where for 33 years I served as a representative. During my time in the legislature, I learned that more than half of the pilots of

the warplanes that flew over Mount Sterling in the '40s were with the Women Airforce Service Pilots (WASP) program, based at Avenger Field in Sweetwater, Texas.

Motivated by patriotism, a love of flying and a keen sense of adventure, the WASPs truly played an important role in World War II, ferrying planes from factories to U.S. air bases, towing gunnery targets, and transporting equipment and personnel, among many other crucial duties. The

WASPs flew every type of plane in the forces.

Cornelia Fort of the Women's Auxiliary Ferrying Squadron, which became part of the WASPs, summed up their contributions in a 1943 essay: "We have no hopes of replacing men pilots. But we can release a man to combat, to faster ships, to overseas work."

Some, including Army Air Forces commander Gen. Henry "Hap" Arnold, doubted at first that women could control the big planes, but the WASPs proved them wrong.

Of the 1,102 women in the WASP program, 38, including Fort, died in the line of duty. The pilots were civilian volunteers, so they were not entitled to military funerals; surviving WASPs would take up collections to have their colleagues' remains sent home.

Sometimes called The Forgotten Air Force, the WASP program was disbanded in December 1944. It was finally granted military status in 1977. And in 2010, each pilot received the Congressional Gold Medal, the highest civilian honor awarded by Congress.

ADRIAN ARNOLD
MOUNT STERLING, KY

VIGILANT AT HOME
My dad, Civil Air Patrol flier Ray Baker, stands by his Waco biplane with my mother, Lucille, also a pilot, myself and brothers Vern and Dale in 1943 outside Detroit, Michigan. Dale and I became pilots, too. White triangles, visible under the wing and near the tail, were the civil patrol's insignia.
BRIAN BAKER · SUN CITY, AZ

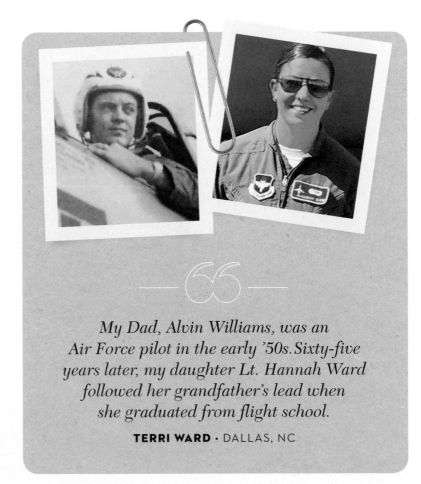

My Dad, Alvin Williams, was an Air Force pilot in the early '50s. Sixty-five years later, my daughter Lt. Hannah Ward followed her grandfather's lead when she graduated from flight school.

TERRI WARD · DALLAS, NC

Ewald met up with Frank Tengler, right, his brother-in-law, while they were in the Pacific theater during World War II. Each man married the other's sister.

Brothers in Arms

Two friends, related by marriage, managed against all odds to reunite during the war.

———

Near the end of 1944, my unit, the 796th Engineer Forestry Battalion, was stationed on Leyte Island near the village of Barrio Buaya in the Philippines, more than 30 miles south of the Army base at Abuyog.

We were completely isolated from Abuyog. There was nothing around us but jungle, mountains and a few villages. Our supplies came by ship across Leyte Gulf.

Throughout the war, my brother-in-law Frank Tengler and I had kept in touch, writing each other at every opportunity. With Frank stationed on a Navy ship in the vastness of the South Pacific and me on land in the same theater, it was remarkable that our letters caught up to us as often as they did. The only time Frank could mail me a letter or pick up his mail was when his ship was in port.

One day in mid-January 1945, I learned that Frank's ship was scheduled to dock at Tacloban, a busy port town north of Abuyog, for a few days in February. He said he'd hitch a ride by Army truck to Abuyog and wait for me to make the long 32-mile trip to meet him. It was an iffy plan at best—and it hinged on perfect timing.

I got the OK for a two-day furlough and waited for Frank's letter telling me which day he'd be in port. When it came, I hired a Buaya resident to take me across the gulf in his outrigger dugout. It was a bit risky—18 miles across open water—but I knew it would save time. Still, no amount of extra money could persuade the man to leave before 2 p.m., which made me very unhappy, as I'd have less time with Frank.

Fortunately, the gulf was calm enough that we reached Abuyog without mishap shortly before dark. After a long search, I heard what I thought was Frank's voice coming out of the darkness.

Frank had been looking for me since he'd arrived around 2 that afternoon. Amazingly, in a base with tens of thousands of GIs, and the dust and noise of constant traffic caused by hundreds of vehicles, we found each other around 9:30 p.m.

Frank and I shot the breeze till way past midnight. After having breakfast together the next morning, we said our goodbyes.

I'd planned to hike back, a daunting 12-hour trek through miles of jungle. Fortunately, the trails were well-marked.

My gear weighed 50 pounds and felt even heavier as I trudged up and down hills, across streams and swamps and through barrios, where the people welcomed me like a hero. I got back to camp well after dark, soaked in sweat, hungry and dead tired—but elated. Frank and I had pulled it off against all odds!

EWALD TIMM · BROOKFIELD, WI

It was an iffy plan at best—and it hinged on perfect timing.

George stands in front of the house he built upon returning to college after WWII. At right, the clock tower at what is now UW-Stout.

POSTWAR BOOM YEAR

MY FUTURE HUSBAND, GEORGE, and I met in 1942 at the beginning of our freshman year at the Stout Institute (now the University of Wisconsin-Stout) in Menomonie, Wisconsin, and we became close friends. By the end of the school year, however, George and the other eligible men on campus had to put their studies on hold to serve in the war. The college student body soon was made up almost entirely of women. We all continued with our studies.

Discharged in 1946, George joined the growing number of veterans returning to (or entering) college on the GI Bill. Back on campus, George rekindled his friendships with prewar buddies and lived in his old dorm. He even was able to room again with his freshman roommate, Robert "Bob" Swanson, who later became chancellor of UW-Stout.

My relationship with George had grown; we'd kept in touch through the war, and after he got home, we decided to marry. Housing was scarce in the small city of Menomonie, so the college built many prefabricated houses, renting them to veterans for $25 per month. We'd hoped to rent one, but shortly before our wedding, we learned that families with children received priority.

Since George's major was industrial arts and my degree was in home economics, our parents encouraged us to build a small home for ourselves. They offered to help with the construction.

Our tiny house was the size of a double garage, yet it became a meeting place where the veterans on campus and others built lasting friendships. George's three best friends found their soul mates at college, and we four couples, all graduates of Stout, became friends for life.

What an impact the GI Bill had on our lives and what wonderful memories!

DOROTHY ZIMMERMAN
MANITOWOC, WI

CALL IT A SMALL REFUND

I lost half a toe during combat in Belgium and entered Cornell University as a disabled veteran on the GI Bill. Along with tuition and fees, I got $110 a month for expenses, but my case had to be reviewed regularly. After another long bus ride and missed classes, I played dumb and asked the VA doctor when my toe would grow back, affecting my eligibility for disability. Of course he said, "Never."

"Then why do I have to keep coming in for these reviews?" He scribbled something in my file, and after that I never had to go back.

I like to think that my question saved the Veterans Administration a lot of money and time over the years, enough, at least, to equal what they paid for my tuition.

BILL HERZOG · ANN ARBOR, MI

WWII vet Don Balfour registers for classes under the GI Bill.

BUILDING A CAREER ON THE GI BILL

I RECEIVED AN EARLY DISCHARGE on Feb. 1, 1946, and enrolled under the GI Bill at the University of Illinois to complete the engineering degree I'd started before entering the service.

I was going back sooner than other GIs, most of whom would not return home from Europe and Asia for months. My bride, Olga, and I had the best choices for housing.

The college had a shortage of professors that year. Because I had an aptitude for structural engineering, I got a job grading homework for the class, which allowed Olga and me to add a little variety to our steady diet of tuna casserole. A few months later, the professor had a heart attack and had to take a long leave. With no one to take his place, the school asked me to teach the course, though I still had to finish my bachelor's degree. Working at the school made it easier to continue my education, so I ended up getting a master's, too.

After I graduated, we moved to Indianapolis, Indiana, where I spent seven years with my family's building construction firm and 11 more in private practice. Later, I was appointed head of building science at Auburn University, where I stayed until I retired in 1993.

What I paid in taxes over the years with my higher professional income more than made up for the cost of my education on the GI Bill. It's one of the smartest things Congress ever did.

PAUL BRANDT
AUBURN, AL

Batting for the Marines

Some celebrities didn't flinch at the
dangers of serving their country.

On Feb. 16, 1953, I was a corporal in the 398th anti-aircraft automatic weapons battalion. We defended K-55 (now Osan Air Base), the big F-86 Sabre jet base near Osan, South Korea.

I was just coming off duty at the communications shed when a signal came over that Boston Red Sox superstar Ted Williams had just crash-landed his Marine Corps F9F Panther jet at the K-13 base near Suwon, about 15 minutes away.

Ted Williams had been one of my heroes since the day in 1941 when he'd handed me a baseball at New York's Yankee Stadium. I was 9 at the time. Little did I know that 12 years later, both he and I would be serving in a war in Korea.

Our base's mail delivery driver knew that I was a big Williams fan, so he invited me to go with him on a mail run to K-13, on the off chance that I might be able to meet the great hitter.

We arrived at the base and immediately saw the disabled Panther. Its nose-mounted 20 mm cannons were bent in half from the wheels-up belly landing. The plane had skidded on the tarmac for almost a mile before coming to a stop, the nose bursting into flames.

Unfortunately, I couldn't meet Ted again at that time—not that he would have remembered me—because he was being treated in the medical unit. I hoped he wasn't badly hurt.

Later it was reported that Williams had limped away from the wreck with a few cuts and bruises but no serious injuries.

The star slugger went home from the war to resume his Hall of Fame career; in fact, he hit a home run in his second at-bat and wound up with a .407 average over 37 games in 1953.

I went home to start a career as a junior clerk with the Great Northern Railroad. I retired 37 years later. I'm still a huge baseball fan.

BILL RAUN · STATEN ISLAND, NY

Bill Raun (near right) poses in
Seoul en route to the base near
Osan, South Korea, in January
1953. Weeks later, Red Sox hitter
Ted Williams crash-landed his
Panther jet practically within
slugging distance of Bill's unit.

Ted Williams had been one of my heroes since the day in 1941 when he'd handed me a baseball at New York's Yankee Stadium.

A Year Older and Wiser

Airman remembers the difficulty of being away, and his relief at coming home.

Just before I shipped out to Vietnam in the summer of 1967, I met a student nurse from Sacramento State College. It was nothing serious—we were friends—but her letters and care packages would come to mean a lot to me over the months when I felt light-years from home.

My one-year tour of duty with the Air Force began in July that year. I was assigned to the 37th Tactical Fighter Wing at Phu Cat Air Base, near the city of Qui Nhon, for two months before moving farther down the coast to join the 35th Tactical Fighter Wing at Phan Rang. There, I was noncommissioned officer in charge of the combat activities reporting center. Our mission was to compile airstrike intelligence data and send it to Seventh Air Force headquarters outside Saigon.

Two weeks before returning stateside, I was on charge-of-quarters duty and listening to Simon and Garfunkel's "The Sounds of Silence" when the base came under mortar attack. Whenever I hear the song now, I remember that night.

I arrived home late on the Fourth of July 1968, landing at McChord Air Force Base near Tacoma, Washington, as the Independence Day fireworks lit up the sky. The next day I was discharged from the Air Force.

It's tough to look back at such a difficult time for our country, which was hard both on those who went to Vietnam and on those at home. But there were moments of kindness that have stayed with me to ease the pain of my memories.

For instance, a year after I got back, I was reading a Tacoma resident's description in *Reader's Digest* of the fireworks that greeted us at McChord, and I learned something I hadn't known at the time. The final part of the display had been delayed until the Freedom Bird I was on landed, to give the soldiers returning from Vietnam a real welcome home. It was a small but thoughtful gesture, and we appreciated it.

DAVID FREIMAN
PALMDALE, CA

David served a year in Vietnam before coming home in July 1968.

THE STORIED SEVENTH AIR FORCE

The Air Force command that ran most of the operations during the Vietnam War has a long history.

Activated as part of the Army Air Corps in November 1940 in Hawaii, it was nicknamed the Pineapple Air Force.

....

Members of the Seventh were the first U.S. airmen to come under hostile enemy fire with the attack on Pearl Harbor.

....

During WWII, it handled heavy-bomber attacks on strategic Pacific locations and escorted long-range B-29s from Iwo Jima, among other duties.

....

After sporadic inactivations, it was revived in 1966 and assumed air combat command at Tan Son Nhut Air Base in Vietnam.

....

It was transferred to Thailand in 1973 to control air operations until it was inactivated two years later.

....

Reactivated in 1986 at Osan Air Base, South Korea, it helps to maintain the armistice with North Korea.

SOURCE: U.S. AIR FORCE

GROOMED FOR SUCCESS

Men's toiletry products catered to
smooth-looking results for customers.

« 1948

Patented Control

Vaseline products went with Commander Peary
to the North Pole and with soldiers to the front
in both world wars. Slicked-back hairstyles of the
'40s called for lots of tonic, but it could dry out
the scalp. Vaseline's cream claimed to soothe
skin and relieve dandruff.

1949 »

Cool and Clean

Another venerable brand—it was celebrating
50 years in business in 1949—Barbasol had been
part of every soldier's standard-issue kit during
WWII. By the mid-1950s, the thick tube version
shown here was replaced by fluffy foam in
aerosol cans, similar to what is sold today.

KIND COMRADERY

ALL SMILES
Female Marine Corps graduates at Camp Pendleton in California enjoy a night out in the 1950s. I'm seated at front left.
ANITA VOGEL HANSON
COLORADO SPRINGS, CO

OVERLAP IN THE ZONE
My husband, Greg, and his twin, Gary, both served in Vietnam. At the time, siblings were not supposed to be assigned to a war zone together, but Greg's and Gary's tours of duty in Cat Lai, Vietnam, in 1970 overlapped by a month. They took advantage of it by spending as much time together as possible. In the pictures, Gary is on the truck and Greg is standing by the jeep; and Greg's on the left at the table.
BETH MONG • EAST AMHERST, NY

TWO IDENTICAL FACES, ONE CONFUSED CLERK

When my father-in-law was drafted into the Army in 1954, his twin volunteered so they could serve together. Coy (left) and Roy Wisecarver caused the mail clerk no end of grief when it came to giving them their letters, as this Army photo shows. Eventually, the clerk got in the habit of handing over all Wisecarver mail to whichever brother showed up. My father-in-law and Roy were honorably discharged as corporals in January 1956.

JIM BRADY · WHITESBURG, TN

IN IT TOGETHER

My father, Loren, poses with his father, David, shortly after WWII. They served in the war at the same time, and at one point both were in the Pacific theater in different branches.

BILL MURPHY · LARGO, FL

Luella McGuire
was a concert
pianist and singer;
her husband,
Carson, was a
Navy surgeon.

Silent Night Vigil

All was calm as she sang of glad tidings
with the voice of an angel.

M y mother, Luella, had such a beautiful voice she was offered a position with the Metropolitan Opera in New York. One Christmas Eve during World War II, as my father headed to the Pacific as a Navy surgeon, my mother volunteered to sing for the troops on a hospital ship anchored at New York Harbor.

The ship had recently returned from Europe with several wounded soldiers. It was obvious they were in serious condition, and some were in great pain.

Mom was moved by the sight of the ailing men, who were worried and saddened to be far from loved ones at the holidays. But she pulled herself together and asked what they wanted to hear. After a long moment, with some shouting, "anything," she started to sing "Silent Night." She finished to a room filled with silence. Finally, someone asked, "Would you sing it again?" She did.

Then she sang it again. And again. Mom guessed she sang "Silent Night" more than 20 times. She

sang with tears in her eyes and a lump in her throat, and she saw that many of the servicemen and medical staff wept, too. My mother would sing for audiences hundreds of times throughout her career, but she always said her performance that night was the most important of her life.

As fate would have it, a few years ago a longtime employee of mine was telling me about his father's experiences as a seaman during the war. His dad vividly recalled the Christmas Eve he spent aboard a hospital ship when an "angel," as he called her, sang "Silent Night" over and over to all of the wounded men.

To say that I was shocked would be an understatement. Later, when shown a picture of my mother, the veteran confirmed that she was his singing angel.

"She touched my heart and the heart of everyone on that ship forever," he said.

TIM McGUIRE
MOUNT MORRIS, IL

Mom guessed she sang "Silent Night" more than 20 times.

New Workforce

Troops rejoice as their ship docks in New York City in August 1945. Many veterans re-entered civilian life with help from the landmark GI Bill.

CHAPTER 7

·························

MOTORING MEMORIES

Unusual cars, family fun and
unexpected twists make travel on
the open road a path to adventure.

Fixer-Upper

I sewed a new top for this beat-up '51 Crosley Hot Shot after I bought
it in 1953. I once had to drive it home in reverse when it got stuck
in gear, but I loved the car anyway. It was perfect for me!

CLAIRE ESPOSITO · MIDDLETOWN, OH

A Ride for the Jet Set

Her family got to test-drive a coveted Chrysler Turbine.

B ack in 1963, when we lived in Raleigh, North Carolina, my dad, Fernando, applied to participate in a Chrysler program. Of the more than 30,000 applicants, he and 202 others were selected to test-drive for three months a new car—the Chrysler Turbine—equipped with a jet-style turbine engine.

I was in first grade and thought the Turbine was the coolest car I'd ever seen. It looked like a vehicle designed for the Jetsons. The body was a gorgeous metallic bronze, and it had a black vinyl hardtop. The upholstery was a luxurious

copper-orange leather and buttery soft. Whenever we went for rides in the Turbine, people openly stared, wondering what kind of car it was. At first I felt awkward with all the attention, but I soon got used to it.

The hump in the middle of the car between the driver and passenger seats extended back between the rear seats to the trunk, and covered part of the turbine engine. I'll never forget the noise the car made when it started up. The loud whir sounded like a jet plane before it takes off.

It may have looked and felt futuristic, but it was still prone to the foibles of ordinary suburban

THE CAR OF THE FUTURE

Writing about the Chrysler Turbine in *Popular Mechanics*, former late-night TV host and classic car buff Jay Leno calls it "the most collectible American car" for its unique design and extreme rarity. Only 55 were made and just nine have survived. Leno owns one of three Turbines that are still drivable. (The two others belong to Chrysler.)

A car with a jet engine was the height of innovation in 1963, even in an era when novel automotive design was common. Chrysler used extended leases to get average drivers' impressions of the vehicle.

"The families who tested the Turbines were treated like rock stars in their towns," Leno writes.

Even so, drivers complained that the Turbine burned fuel too quickly, and they didn't like having to hunt for the smelly diesel the car needed. After 27 months, Chrysler ended the test drives and chose not to bring the Turbine to market.

- Chrysler experimented with turbine concept cars from the early 1950s to the late 1980s.

- With modifications, the engine could run on anything flammable. A Chrysler Turbine on a world tour in 1964 had a stop in Mexico, where President Adolfo Mateos drove it on a tank of tequila.

- Introducing the Turbine, Chrysler listed its advantages over piston-engine cars, including long engine life, fewer moving parts, instant cabin heat in winter, no engine vibration, and cool, clean exhaust.

- The Turbine's mostly foreign-made parts meant that Chrysler would've had to pay import fees on the pilot test cars after it stopped the lease program. The carmaker avoided this by junking 46 of the original 55 Turbines. The survivors landed in private collections or museums.

Mary's family, Mom Dora and brothers David (left) and Martin, turned heads when they cruised in the Turbine.

driving. Mom had a close call one day when she was backing it out of the garage. Our driveway sloped down toward the house, creating a blind spot, so she didn't see our 1959 Plymouth Savoy parked right behind the Turbine, and she hit it. To everyone's relief there was no damage to the Turbine and only a minor ding to the Savoy.

I was sad to see the car go when our three-month lease was up. But I'll always remember the experience and the special part we played in automotive history.

MARY JOHNSON · BELTSVILLE, MD

Evelyn surprised husband Bryant with this pretty new Ford (top) when he was discharged in 1946. The Ford was still going strong when Bryant posed next to it with dog Fleet in 1949.

Off-Roading Lesson

The ocean almost swallowed up their fun.

———

Neither Bryant nor I had ever owned a car—few young people could afford one in the late '30s and early '40s. But when the war ended in 1945, domestic auto production picked up, so it was a good time to buy. Before our husbands were discharged from the Army, my sister-in-law and I decided to attend the opening of a Ford dealership to see the first models made for peacetime.

The evening of the opening it poured rain, but we set out anyway, and we were the only ones who showed up. The dealer gave us his full attention, and we each wound up ordering a car.

About a week before Bryant came home, our Ford arrived, the first postwar one delivered in LeRoy. It was a glorious moment when I took Bryant out to the garage and surprised him with our new dark blue two-door, eight-cylinder Ford.

We immediately took it out for a drive. In his exuberance, Bryant honked the horn so much it stuck. My husband was no mechanic, but after a few haphazard knocks under the hood, he got the thing to quit blaring.

A week later, we started on a road trip to Florida. Wherever we drove, people stopped in their tracks to stare at us and wave. We were an oddity in this new world of peace.

We stayed in Daytona to see the car races and I drove for a stretch along the beach. As I turned to take us back, our front tires sank into the sand. Bryant tried, but the car sank even deeper. We stood there on the empty beach, uncertain what to do, when a boy on his bike warned us that the tide was coming in. The week before, he said, a car had sunk out of sight at high tide.

Frantic, Bryant ran for help while I was left to pace around the car as the Atlantic lapped ever nearer. I don't know how long it was—it seemed an eternity—before I saw Bryant running toward me with six sailors he'd found in a bar. They quickly pushed us onto terra firma.

The rest of our journey of 3,000-plus miles went quite smoothly. Back in LeRoy, Bryant took the car in for a checkup at the dealership, where everyone was amazed that we hadn't had any maintenance on it, not even an oil change, in all those miles.

I told you Bryant was no mechanic!

EVELYN TAYLOR · LeROY, NY

The Prodigal Coupe

They sold it, but their son bought it back.

When my husband, Tom, drove our brand-new Oldsmobile 4-4-2 Holiday coupe into my parents' yard in 1969, Dad was not pleased. He thought a station wagon would have been a more sensible choice, seeing as how we had one young son and another on the way.

After we drove it for four years and the boys got bigger, we realized Dad was right—it wasn't a family car. We sold it to a neighbor, who drove it for a few years more before storing it.

When our oldest son, Scott, turned 16 and got his license, he wanted a Camaro, but Tom said "no way." Scott didn't talk to his father for several days, but he had birthday and summer-job money burning a hole in his pocket, and he was determined to buy a car. One day we came home and saw our old coupe sitting in the driveway;

Scott had bought it back from our neighbor. Tom still had a soft spot for his old muscle car, so he helped Scott restore it to good running condition.

When Scott went off to college, we bought the car back from him and continued the restoration work. Until Tom passed away in 2017, he thrilled to the sound of the engine's roar and the feel of that powerful car. It still has a home in my garage, never to see rain or snow.

The coupe nearly came to an early end in 1971. Tom was at work that day and saw it all through a window: In a parking lot at the top of a nearby hill, the brakes on a pickup failed and the vehicle rolled down a 50-foot embankment, landing on our car and crushing the roof. A body shop brought it back to its original glory.

BARBARA MYERS · HATFIELD, MA

Scott relaxes with his two favorite pets—his cat and the '69 Olds.

ON THE WAGON

The long and the short of the vehicle built for families.

1958 »

Long on Glamour

The station wagon was an American staple by the mid-1950s. Olds sought to set its Super 88 Fiesta apart by calling it "glamorous" and "versatile," which may explain why Jerry Lewis is promoting it here; the popular comedian, who also sang and danced, was seen as a star who could do it all.

MEET YOUR NEW DIMENSION
IN STATION WAGONS—
FOR FAMILY WORK 'N' FUN

THE *LARK* PLAY WAGON BY STUDEBAKER

Here's the newest, happiest, fam'liest wagon of all—a whole *new dimension* in wagons—with a full, big 93 cu. ft. cargo space nestled neatly on a tidy 113-inch wheelbase. Far shorter outside than conventional wagons—far easier to handle, turn and park. Far more economical, too—with either the economy six or super V-8 engine delivering top mileage, peak performance, on regular low-cost gas. Beautifully built and engineered. Styled with unique flair, rich in fine finishing touches, upholstered in handsome, practical vinyl. Optional rear-facing hideaway seat brings capacity up to eight passengers. Smart, sensible, spirited, it costs less to buy, far less to operate. It's the one women love, children adore, men go for. Look at, price, drive, compare *The Lark* Play Wagon *by Studebaker* at your dealer's today. It's the welcomest wagon of all!

Also 2-door and 4-door sedan and hardtop.

« 1958

Playing for Time

As Studebaker-Packard was going through yet another financial turmoil, it introduced the Lark line for the 1959 model year, marketing the cars as compact, economical alternatives to typical station wagon behemoths. This ad boasts that the Play Wagon is "far shorter" than other wagons but offers 93 cubic feet of cargo space. Larks kept the company afloat before it finally closed U.S. operations in 1963.

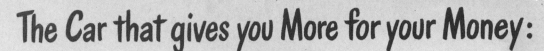

The Car that gives you More for your Money:

- A Roomy, Comfortable Passenger Car...

It's level-riding on any road... with ample room for six people, plus big luggage space, in its all-steel body. You'll like this nimble car's driving ease, too—its light, quick steering response... short turning radius... the safer vision of large, deep windows all around.

MORE MILEAGE AND LESS UPKEEP

The famous 'Jeep' Engine with fuel-stretching overdrive gives mileage that saves you money. You'll appreciate, too, the fine maintenance service you get from Willys-Overland dealers, and the low cost of parts and repairs.

... and a Utility Vehicle, too

The 'Jeep' Station Wagon gives you the extra value of double usefulness. Seats are easily removable to provide space for hauling bulky loads. See a Willys-Overland dealer for the car that delivers more for your money!

'Jeep' Station Wagon

A REALLY NEW KIND OF CAR...

The 'Jeep' Station Sedan combines the luxurious riding ease of a sedan with the spaciousness of a station-wagon. Its finely appointed interior gives passengers extraordinary headroom and legroom. Its 6-cylinder engine, with overdrive, assures top performance and long fuel mileage.

'Jeep' Station Sedan

WILLYS-OVERLAND MOTORS, TOLEDO 1, OHIO • MAKERS OF AMERICA'S MOST USEFUL VEHICLES

1950   **A Utility Vehicle for Everyone**

Willys-Overland's Jeep wagon, introduced in 1946, competed favorably with Detroit makers' wood-sided wagons by offering four-wheel drive, removable seats for more storage and an almost indestructible steel body. It proved to be the company's most popular model.

Homemade Gem
Blazed a Trail

First it was a travel camper, then a cool pad for the kids.

Born in Oregon in 1949, I was the second of four children. Our dad, Allen, was a white-collar worker; Mom, Bernice, was a part-time night nurse. Because they worked different shifts, we seldom had a baby sitter.

Nice recreational toys such as boats, planes and travel trailers were uncommon then and out of reach for most people except the well-to-do. Mom and Dad were not in that league. However, like lots of parents back then, they improvised. Dad was good with his hands and had accumulated many tools.

In the mid-1950s, a big new grocery store was going up in our town and the refrigeration equipment was delivered to the site packed in oak crates. The builders allowed Dad to take away all of this discarded wood.

Over time, my father also acquired an old trailer frame, upholstered seats from a remodeled restaurant, a sink, and other things from secondhand stores.

Finally, it was time for him to start building the family's travel trailer. It took him several months, but by the next year, we were towing our homemade trailer to different camping sites in Oregon. And what

Dressy campers Patti, Scott and Bob, with Bernice (Mom) and Ken, pose next to the trailer built by Allen (Dad) in this color image from 1955.

At Oregon's Breitenbush campground in 1957, the trailer rolls behind the family's 10-year-old Cadillac. "I do not remember Dad ever buying a new car," Scott says.

a conversation piece it turned out to be—complete with a working sink, lights, closet and enough room for all six of us.

Dad and Mom never owned more than a three-bedroom home. With four growing children in the house by the mid-1960s, Dad's travel trailer became a needed fourth bedroom for my brother Bob, the eldest. A few years later, once Bob had left for the Marines, I inherited the trailer to use as my bedroom.

Eventually, I went into the Army and the family had no further need for the trailer. Dad finally sold it.

I often wonder what became of the homemade camper that served our family well for so many years. I hope whoever bought it enjoyed it as much as we did.

SCOTT SUTHERLAND
PLEASANT VIEW, UT

Bob and Scott play by the oak crates their dad used to build the camper.

THE TRAVELING SET

SEEING THE COUNTRY BY TRAVEL TRAILER

was a national pastime at midcentury. Enthusiasts called themselves "trailerites" or "tin can tourists" at a time when suburban households boasted big cars that could handily tow a 3,000-pound camper.

The trailer market was fierce: A 1949 *Billboard* ad lists models from 55 manufacturers. The Kozy Coach Co. in Kalamazoo, Michigan, adopted the slogan "You're Ahead with a Kozy Coach Behind," and set its models apart with superior materials like polished woods and homey touches like glass-front kitchen cabinets. Its deluxe model sold for $765 in 1936—almost $14,000 today. Kozy Coaches and other extinct trailer brands are collectors items now.

SMALL-SCALE LUXURY IN A 1949 DELUXE KOZY COACH

1. Weathertight trailers could get stuffy; a vent above the propane stove was a must. The kitchen area had plenty of storage. **2.** Polished birch was an attractive choice for a dinette; table and bench tucked into wall nooks by folding up the legs. **3.** The roomy sofa pulled out into a double bed. **4.** Some deluxe models included baths with showers.

The Sclafanis, Evelyn, Ernestine, Jay and Joyce, relied on John, above, to handle the testy VW bus.

Long, Slow Roll Down the Mountain

How do you back up with no transmission? Very carefully.

———

Mount Snow never looked so frightening as it did when the transmission on our old Volkswagen bus failed that dreadful morning in August 1964.

In the middle of our monthlong camping vacation in Vermont, we were taking a friendly day trip up the mountain. But in a flash, things had suddenly gone very, very wrong.

Dad slammed on the brakes as gray smoke and the inky odor of transmission fluid filled the vehicle's interior. My sister Joyce and I, 11 and 9, were glued to the back window, watching our impending doom as the VW skidded down the unpaved road. Our little sister Ernestine, 4, was still relatively calm, but for an occasional shriek.

Only an hour earlier, we'd all been laughing and singing songs in the bright summer morning. Now all we could do was stare out the window in panic.

Seeing the loose rocks and dirt cascading to the forest floor far below us, our mother was a bundle of nerves. "Maybe we can call for help?" she asked.

"Do you see a phone booth anywhere?" Dad growled. "Now everybody shut up—I need to concentrate." He threw it in neutral and maneuvered the bus inch by inch in reverse,

a white-knuckle grip on the steering wheel and sweat pouring from his brow.

We crept down the barren winding road, the only sounds coming from the creaking chassis and the brakes groaning against the pull of gravity.

There was no shoulder or even a clearing where Dad could turn the vehicle around. We continued to roll slowly backward, no one daring to make a sound—except Ernestine.

"I have to go to the bathroom," she announced matter-of-factly, and held up her doll to show us. "So does Barbie."

Our mother shushed her and shot a sidelong glance at Dad. But he took no notice—he was twisted at a grotesque angle, his eyes on the track.

Finally, after what seemed like hours, we backed up to the entrance. We'd not seen another soul the whole way down. Dad maneuvered the bus to a clearing, set the emergency brake and let out a long, pent-up breath. Drenched in sweat, he smiled nervously at Mom, who gently patted his still-trembling hand.

"You did it, John," she said. "You are the king of this mountain."

J.P. SCLAFANI · PORT JEFFERSON, NY

Bill stands next to Nellie Bell before the big trip. The 1960 Morris Oxford Traveller had a top speed of 75 mph, according to the maker. But perhaps it didn't go that fast while packed to the roof for a tour through one province and nine states.

Nellie Bell Got Them There

British import was up to challenge of the American West.

Originally from Glasgow, Scotland, my parents and I immigrated to Canada in 1956, when I was 4. We lived in Hamilton, Ontario, until 1963, when we moved to wintery Winnipeg, Manitoba.

We were in Winnipeg just a year before my parents decided to try out sunny Milpitas, California, on the advice of friends who had already made the move. I was only 11 at the time, but the trip left indelible memories.

After sorting out all the documentation, which included having our fingerprints taken by the Royal Canadian Mounted Police, the three of us set out in the trusty 1960 Morris Oxford station wagon that we'd named Nellie Bell. We'd sent our furniture ahead by truck; the Morris was packed to the roof with the rest of our belongings.

But we did manage to rig up a small bed for me behind the front seats.

It was a cold day in November 1964 when we reached the U.S.-Canada border at North Dakota. We wanted to see the sights, so we followed a route that took us through several states. We roamed steadily south and west through South

We enjoyed life in the Golden State, but our family was still back in Hamilton and we missed them.

Dakota, Nebraska, Kansas and Oklahoma, before hitting the glorious warmer climes of Texas, New Mexico and Arizona.

Seeing the desert for the first time was an amazing experience. Dad wanted to preserve the memory with a photo and had my mother stand in front of a giant cactus. He kept asking her to back up a bit, which she did—without looking—until the spiky plant made a painful impression on her.

After a week of traveling, we finally reached Los Angeles, with its bewildering multilevel freeways, then made our way up to Milpitas near San Jose, where we settled in just around the corner from our friends.

We enjoyed life in the Golden State, but our family was still back in Hamilton and we missed them. So the day Mum walked into the living room and asked "hands up all who want to move back to Canada," our fate was set.

Less than two years after our great move south, the three of us were back in the Morris wagon heading north.

We sold Nellie Bell about a year after we had returned to Hamilton. Imagine our amazement just a few years later when she showed up at a garage down the road from us! She had found us once again.

BILL SMILLIE · GRIMSBY, ON

The Smillies took several days to drive more than 2,500 miles to California in their Morris, stopping frequently to take in the sights. At top, Bill and his mother, Helen, at historic Boothill in Tombstone, Arizona. Above, Bill Sr. and son at the New Mexico border.

NICE WHEELS!

« PICTURE PERFECT
The Packard proving grounds in Utica, Michigan, was the setting for this glamour shot of a 1941 One-Twenty Touring Sedan. My father, company photographer George Collick, took the photo. Everyone in the picture was a model except the little boy—that's my brother Garfield Collick, who was 4 at the time.
ELLEN LUCY · HALE, MI

DUNE BUGGY DREAM ⌄
My daughter Gail wasn't thrilled when I brought home a VW wreck to be her first car in 1968. But after I stripped it down and put a new Meyers Manx dune buggy body on it, Gail became a bit more enthused. We were living on California's Alameda Island, where her car was a big hit.
ROY NICHOLS · RENO, NV

Me and my 1967 Camaro RS/SS, which I've owned for more than 46 years. It swings a lot of heads when I drive by.

JOAN GERBER · CAMDEN, NY

THANKS, DAD!

I got my first car, a 1962 Chevy, while finishing college in Stevens Point, Wisconsin, in 1972. I needed a car to do my practice teaching in Portage, and my dad bought it for me for $100.

KATHRYN RIDDER
CHILTON, WI

SUNDAY DRIVE

My mom, Phyllis Merrill, poses with her 1939 Buick Special near Oakland, California, in 1941. My dad, Richard, would buy her a new car every two years. I still drive the Mercury Monterey ragtop Dad and Mom gave me in 1959.

JAY JUNE FINLAY · SUN CITY WEST, AZ

In Brockton, Massachusetts, Charlie, left, Jack, second from left, and Bill, right, pose with their friend Louie.

Destination: Maine or Bust

Three friends take to the open road in a rickety Model A.

Before the start of our fall semester at Purdue University in 1947, my good friends John "Jack" Irvine, William "Bill" Brown and I decided to take a road trip from Indiana to Maine.

We bought an aging 1929 Ford Model A for $90, painted "Maine or Bust" on each door, and named the heap Mary Jo after our girlfriends at the time.

Leaving West Lafayette, Indiana, on Aug. 26, we stopped for coffee in Huntington, Indiana, where a local newspaper reporter interviewed us for a story. It was such fun that for the rest of the trip we'd contact the local paper whenever we passed through a sizable town. It helped that we were traveling only two years after World War II, when it was still a novelty to see an out-of-state license plate far from home.

We managed to hit places on our route where we had relatives or friends willing to put us up, feed us a good meal and spot us a few dollars for gas and groceries. We roughed it, too, when we had to.

Our worst experience was getting lost in western Pennsylvania and ending up at a condemned bridge over the Allegheny River. We crossed at night, with one of us walking in front of the car looking for holes in the planking. Once safely on the other side, we slung Navy hammocks between pines in the Allegheny National Forest for our beds.

Mary Jo had a top speed of 65 mph and averaged about 19 mpg. She was a jalopy, but reliable—until she broke down on New York's Long Island. Fortunately, a mechanic installed new bearings and got us running. We renamed the car Mary Jo Jones in his honor.

We reached Maine on Sept. 2, and the *Portland Press Herald* ran a feature on us. Still eager to explore, we headed to Canada. In Montreal, we met three young women who spoke only French, although it was clear they were enamored of Mary Jo Jones.

It took us three more days to get home, where we judged the trip a success: 3,000 miles, no traffic tickets and total expenses of $19 each. And we sold the Model A for a profit.

For years afterward, the three of us would get together to relive every mile—while our wives retreated to another room.

CHARLES KLINGER · VENICE, FL

Rest Stop

L. Wing (right), a Metz vehicle agent, stands next to the
Model 22 Speedster he drove from Los Angeles, California, into
the Grand Canyon and back in 1914. With him is LA reporter
O.K. Parker, who chronicled the 1,400-mile journey.

CHAPTER 8

SEEING STARS

Fascinating chance encounters
with celebrities, and Hollywood
appeal at its best.

Shot on Location

Our dad, Dick Merrill, hugs my sister Marilyn and me, 13 and 11, on the Warner Bros. backlot in Burbank, California, in 1953. The studio didn't have public tours then but would show VIPs like the queen around. Ordinary people could get in if they knew an employee. A commercial artist, Dad probably had contacts in the animation studio.

JAY JUNE FINLAY • SUN CITY WEST, AZ

At left, legendary director Alfred Hitchcock gives Robert Burks, the film's director of photography, angle pointers. Below, Hitchcock discusses the merchandise with a candy store clerk.

Hitchcock Thriller

They skipped school for a lesson in master filmmaking.

As juniors at Lane Tech High School in Chicago, Illinois, in 1958, my friend Joe Danford and I were huge movie fans and shot our own 8 mm films, hoping one day to get into the business. So when Alfred Hitchcock arrived in Chicago to shoot scenes for *North by Northwest*, we cut school and went down to the LaSalle Street Station to watch.

The station was packed with people trying to get a glimpse of Hitchcock or any of the movie's three stars: Cary Grant, Eva Marie Saint and James Mason. There was also a tall actor with dark hair who I thought was Cary Grant's stand-in. Later, when I saw the finished movie, I realized it was Martin Landau, who played one of the villains.

Joe and I got as close to the shooting crew as we could without causing any problems. Most of them were friendly, and when we explained that we were doing an article about the shoot for our high school magazine (true), they didn't mind us hanging around as long as we stayed out of the way.

We stood next to the huge VistaVision camera as the crew shot crowd scenes using hundreds of extras. Each extra wore a red or green tag and never appeared in a scene twice. For this, they were paid $18.50 for a 12-hour day.

While the assistant director got the crew and extras ready for the next scene, Hitchcock was only a few feet away, discussing how to improve the shot with Robert Burks, his director of photography.

*A lot of scenes had to be reshot because
of technical problems or because fans got in the way,
but it was all great fun to watch.*

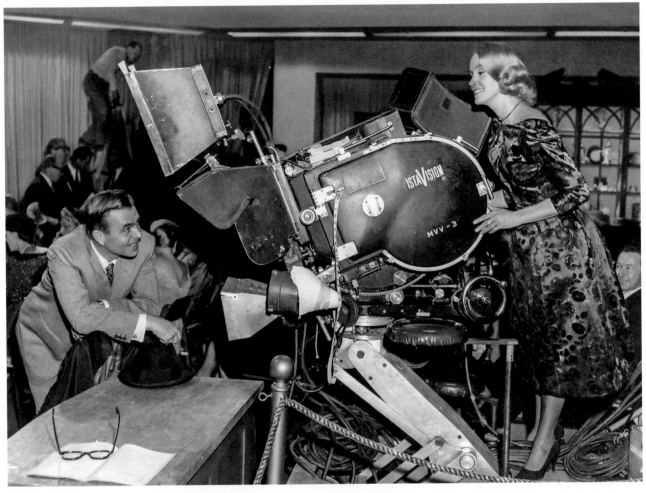

James Mason and Eva Marie Saint pose during a PR event for *North by Northwest* in 1959.

When all was ready, the assistant director called out: "Places, everyone. This will be a take." Then came the roar: "Action!"

Across from us, Cary Grant walked out of a small room, looked around and disappeared into the crowd of extras. It had taken an hour to set up the shot and it was over in a minute. Later we watched as Eva Marie Saint, having just spoken to Martin Landau on the telephone, stepped out of a long row of phone booths. Then came the scene in which police race though the train station, searching for Grant among a dozen redcap porters.

A lot of scenes had to be reshot because of technical problems or because fans got in the way, but it was all great fun to watch.

Joe and I followed Hitchcock—the crew called him Hitch—as much as possible. He was often surrounded by publicity people, press photographers and fans, but he never once got upset. In fact, I think he enjoyed all the adoration and played his role to a T, even posing for some silly publicity photos at a candy shop.

Now every time I watch *North by Northwest*, I remember exactly where I was standing, where the lights were and where the camera was set up during each of the scenes I saw filmed the day I got to see Alfred Hitchcock in action.

DENNIS S. JOHNSON · MENA, AR

Frankly, My Dear…

Gracious movie legend creates an unforgettable moment.

The year was 1952, and I was 24 years old. My husband, Bill, and I were driving from Kentucky to El Monte, California, to visit my aunt. As we were motoring around Encino, California, looking at a map of the stars' homes, we happened to pass by Clark Gable's house. Imagine our surprise when we saw the movie star standing at his mailbox.

"There he is!" I shouted, and made Bill back up.

By that time, however, Gable had climbed back into his Jeep.

"Excuse me," I said to him. "Could I take your picture, please?"

It wouldn't have fazed me if he had decided to drive away. But instead, he looked around, and in that unmistakable Clark Gable drawl, he replied, "I don't see why not, honey."

Clark got out of the Jeep and insisted on including me in the photo. "Come on over here," he said. "I won't bite."

What a wonderful day and a fantastic memory to carry with me through all these years. My daughter even took the picture to school years later for show and tell.

PEGGY GENTRY · CLEARWATER, FL

After a chance meeting outside Clark Gable's house, Peggy was thrilled when the Oscar winner offered to pose for a picture with her.

Best Assignment Ever

Her school paper sent her to report on Gregory Peck.

Ruggedly handsome Gregory Peck was one of the most famous Hollywood actors back in 1947. In the fall of that year, he had just finished filming *Gentleman's Agreement* and was currently on stage in San Francisco starring in *Angel Street*, better known as *Gaslight*. And I, a senior at Fremont High School in Oakland, California, was an editor on the school paper.

During that era, the *Oakland Tribune* regularly included a supplement called the *Teen-Times* in which high school journalists were assigned to write feature articles for the newspaper. Two major celebrities in the Bay Area—Gregory Peck and a popular bandleader, Spike Jones—had agreed to meet and give interviews to high school reporters.

You can guess who my first choice was. After some cajoling, I was assigned to interview Gregory Peck at the Fairmont Hotel.

What an exciting day it was when photographer, Damon Nalty, and I embarked on a public bus for San Francisco—and on a school day at that! We entered the hotel and checked in at the front desk, where the clerk said that Mr. Peck was expecting us. One knock on the door, and there he was, smiling and inviting us in.

Mr. Peck was thoughtful, kind and patient, and shared many wonderful stories with us. After the interview, Mrs. Greta Peck called room service for refreshments before we began our journey back to Oakland. It was one of the most unforgettable days of my life.

But that's not the end of the story. In 1996, I was retired from teaching and living in Modesto. My son Terry read that Gregory Peck would be speaking at U.C. Berkeley in February, and he got four almost-front-row seats for the event. I took along one of the original photos from my interview, just in case.

My husband, Bill, and I were invited backstage after the program finished. Mr. Peck signed my photograph—"For Lillian, After all, Love from Gregory Peck." He also signed Terry's copy of the comic book *Moby Dick*, where Peck appears on the cover as Captain Ahab.

Few young people today recognize the name Gregory Peck. But if you mention *To Kill a Mockingbird*, many will remember the man who played Atticus Finch—and Mr. Peck's face.

LILLIAN KARLOTSKI ALLEN
MODESTO, CA

What Are the Odds?

His friend had more than one connection to Fess Parker.

While in the Army, I was stationed for a time at Fort Sill, Oklahoma, as a field artillery fire direction adviser. In the summer of 1955, our team was sent to assist at a National Guard and Reserve summer encampment at Camp Breckinridge, Kentucky. The *Disneyland* TV series was filming episodes of its popular *Davy Crockett* in the area at the time.

As luck would have it, one afternoon when my friend and team member Tucker Smith and I were in the nearby town of Morganfield, we ran into Fess Parker, the actor who played Davy Crockett on the show.

Tucker started a conversation with the actor and learned they had both attended the same university in Texas. When Fess asked where we were from, we made another discovery: It turned out that both he and Tucker had dated the same girl from Tucker's hometown of Little Rock, Arkansas.

Fess was delightfully friendly, and when we asked him if he would mind if we took a picture, he generously agreed. I wanted the photo to send to my young nephews, who were huge Davy Crockett fans. But I needed one more favor of the actor. I asked him to stand in the gutter next to the curb so I wouldn't look so short next to him. At 6 foot 5, Fess Parker was a good 8 to 10 inches taller than me. In other words, he was one tall man.

GENE WATSON · MESA, AZ

Standing tall, Gene, at left and on the curb, poses with actor Fess Parker, who played Disney's Davy Crockett.

Henry Winkler played it cool as The Fonz on *Happy Days*, but he was a total sweetheart to Terri backstage.

Oh Happy Day!

Memorable favor from Arthur "Fonzie" Fonzarelli himself.

———

Growing up in Norco, California, in the '60s and '70s had its perks. I experienced one of them at age 14 when my boyfriend at the time got a small part in a movie and invited me and my older sister to go with him to the Hollywood set.

We watched him shoot an airport scene for the movie *Baby Blue Marine* (1976), starring Jan-Michael Vincent.

Walking back to our car after the filming, we noticed a line of people going into another set. We asked around and learned that it was the location of the TV show *Happy Days*.

Of course, we had to get in on that! But we didn't have tickets, so we were stuck outside. I was very upset and unable to hide my disappointment.

At that point, I heard someone approaching. "What's the matter?" he asked.

I was surprised to see that it was actor Henry Winkler (aka Arthur "Fonzie" Fonzarelli). He'd been on his way to the set when he stopped to talk to us.

"They won't let us in," I said with a pout.

Amused, The Fonz kissed my forehead, put his arm around me and said, "I'll get you in." He then escorted the three of us through a side door and asked that we "keep this between us." As we passed the woman who had previously turned us away, he told her, "These are personal friends of mine."

We were ushered to the bleachers, where we were able to watch the fascinating inner workings of a TV show filmed before a live studio audience.

Seeing all the stars was a treat. The most memorable scene involved Fonzie watching over a group of boys, one of whom had to spray The Fonz with a squirt gun. They had to do multiple takes because Winkler kept anticipating the squirt and closing his eyes.

After the show, I went down to the set to see Winkler to thank him for his kindness before we left. He smiled and winked as we walked out.

That special memory, sealed with a kiss, will be with me—and will be something I can brag about—for the rest of my life.

TERRI WARD · DALLAS, NC

In high school, John Belushi, far right, played drums in a band with Phil Special on organ and Dick Blasucci holding the bass guitar.

Big Personality Left a Lasting Impression

Making others laugh was a Belushi family gift.

E ven in his early years, John Belushi was a funny guy. I went to Wheaton Central High School in Wheaton, Illinois, where I was two years ahead of him. John and I participated every spring in the high school talent show, so I got to see him in action. It was a lot of work with nightly rehearsals, but so much fun.

One year, John did a stand-up comedy routine, possibly his first. He wore all leather and rode a motorcycle on stage. Then he performed a routine he had written. The entire ensemble thought he was hilarious.

When I was a senior in 1965, I was a soloist and performed with the orchestra under the direction of our teacher, Mr. Gansman. John was a sophomore that year and played drums in a three-piece band. For a short while, my brother Paul was in the band with John, who would come over to our house often to practice.

His older sister, Marian, also a senior, was in my class. The younger Belushi brother, Jim, was just a kid when I knew him.

Agnes Belushi, their mother, took bridge lessons with my mother in 1964. Mom said Agnes was one of the funniest women she ever knew. It seems that wonderful gift of making people laugh began with Agnes.

John's dad was an Albanian immigrant and owned a burger place in Chicago. He worked there all week and many times was only home on the weekend. He talked very much like John did in his *Saturday Night Live* skit serving up "cheezborga, cheezborga, cheezborga."

Our family was blessed to have known the Belushi family and to have enjoyed their remarkable humor.

PEGGY CARNEY GENTRY
GREAT FALLS, MT

BEAUTY'S SECRETS

Is it in the make-up, or the gum? A star's allure is sure worth emulating.

« 1947

Packed with Glam

Big makers like Wrigley and Beech-Nut saw their dominance of the so-called "nickel gum" trade fall with wartime shortages of sugar and other ingredients. Right after the war, smaller "penny gum" makers moved in on the $90 million market with ambitious ad campaigns. Here, Bowman Gum links its Warrens Mint Cocktail with Hollywood's dazzling lifestyle.

1947 »

Hooray for Hollywood

Max Factor perfected the Hollywood look with Pan-Cake Make-Up, a luminous creamy powder that made faces look "natural" in the age of gaudy Technicolor. As women everywhere dreamed of looking like a movie star, Max Factor used its credibility among the famous to create a series of ads featuring fresh-faced actresses, including this one with *Summer Holiday*'s Marilyn Maxwell.

Thanks for the Watermelons

Devoted fans brought Bob Hope a taste of Missouri.

The great watermelon tradition started long before I got involved. During his vaudeville days, a hoofer named Bob Hope found himself at the best-known watermelon stand in St. Louis, Missouri, buying one of the big, juicy summertime fruits. He told the fruit vendor, Sam Zvibleman, that the Midwest melons tasted much better than those grown in California. Both agreed that watermelons were nature's noblest fruit.

For two decades, as Hope's career grew, Sam the Watermelon Man sent a watermelon to the entertainer's dressing room whenever he was in town. He also drove a carload of the beloved watermelons to his now friend in Burbank, California, every year.

In 1958 Hope was playing in the musical *Roberta* at the St. Louis Municipal Opera Theatre. Sam delivered the goods there as usual, but he handed over the yearly California drive to a younger friend, Joe Bornstein. And Joe did it for many years afterward.

July 1974 marked Joe's 17th annual watermelon trip. That's when I came in. Joe was dating my mother, Betty, and he invited us to join him on the trek.

I had just graduated from high school, so I went with them. We drove a car donated by a local car dealership, which also sponsored and advertised the event.

That year, along with the three of us and our belongings, we loaded 17 watermelons into the back of the station wagon and drove cross-country to deliver the precious cargo.

What a thrill it was when we finally got to the house and Bob Hope came out to greet us. He was just as excited about all of the watermelons we brought as we were to be there delivering the bounty.

KATHY ROBINSON · IMPERIAL, MO

Delivering watermelons to Bob Hope was an annual event. Kathy, above center, made the trip with her mom from Missouri to California in 1974.

Einstein's home in Princeton is now a historic landmark.

It Was a Genius Move

He took a chance and met the great Albert Einstein.

———

Annual tuition in 1942 at Princeton University in New Jersey was $450, a financial stretch for my dad, so I worked as a waiter in the dining halls for my board. At the end of my first year, I took a leave of absence and enlisted in the service along with about two-thirds of my classmates. I was ordered to the Stevens Institute of Technology in Hoboken, about 50 miles away, for further studies under the Navy's V-12 officer training program.

One Sunday in June 1944, during a liberty break from studies and drills, I borrowed my father's car and drove back to Princeton to visit friends still on campus. One regret I had from my time as a student there was that I'd never seen Albert Einstein. He lived in town and worked at the Institute for Advanced Study. Camera in hand, I ventured to his home at 112 Mercer St.

Locating the house was no problem. On a whim, I crossed the street and knocked on the door. A housekeeper answered the door, and I asked if Dr. Einstein lived there. She assured me he did and invited me in. She led me to the study and introduced Professor Einstein.

He looked exactly like his photos—gray-white unkempt hair, Teddy Roosevelt mustache, wrinkled sweatshirt, sad but twinkling eyes, baggy pants, sandals, curled pipe in hand. Papers and books were piled on shelves, tables and chairs everywhere. He cleared a space and motioned for me to sit down, asking if I would like to join him for some tea and crumpets. I said yes, of course.

I don't recall being nervous in his presence. It was like having a conversation with my beloved German grandfather. Though he had a heavy accent, I could easily understand him. He put me completely at ease and asked about the math courses I was taking at the time.

I spent the rest of the afternoon with the man who became *Time*'s Person of the Century and the only individual in history immediately associated with and identifiable by a simple equation.

Over the years, I've read about his life, his accomplishments, his humility, his wise philosophy and his humorous anecdotes. His place in history is unchallenged. His shining place in my memory will never dim.

DICK BOERA · ESSEX JUNCTION, VT

Stardust Memories

His bandleader father performed with Dale Evans and Frank Sinatra.

———

My father, Austin Mansfield, was bandleader and guitarist with a group called the Aristocrats of Rhythm before World War II. He and his band often played the Balinese Room of the elegant Blackstone Hotel in Chicago, Illinois, where singer Dale Evans sometimes joined as a soloist. This was a few years before she met and married Roy Rogers.

During the war, Dad was a sergeant in the Army Air Corps stationed at Mitchel Field in Long Island, New York, as a liaison pilot. He belonged to the Mitchel Field choir, which performed with Frank Sinatra at Carnegie Hall in September 1943 as part of the kickoff for the Third War Loan campaign.

I still have the letter W. Randolph Burgess, New York chairman of the War Finance Committee, sent my father thanking him for his "splendid and ... marked contribution to our program," which was broadcast on CBS Radio. The U.S. Treasury raised close to $19 billion in that three-week war bonds drive.

Dad pursued his music for a few years after the war, traveling all around the country with my mother, two brothers and me. Eventually we settled down in Minnesota, where my dad became a corporate pilot.

MIKE MANSFIELD
DELTONA, FL

Austin Mansfield, with guitar, and his band do a show with singer Dale Evans in Chicago.

Mitchel Field choristers sing with Frank Sinatra, center, in 1943 to kick off a war bond drive. Austin is at the far left.

ALL FIRED UP FOR THE BOYS

During the winter of 1951 I spent weeks on the front line in Korea as a forward observer directing fire for the 39th Field Artillery Battalion. Eventually, my crew and I were sent to battalion headquarters in Chorwon Valley for R&R. While there, I snapped a few pictures of actors Betty Hutton and Paul Douglas, who were on a USO tour. I marveled at the time how unconcerned they were to be within shelling distance of the front line. Here is Betty setting off a howitzer.

ERNIE OGREN
TORRANCE, CA

Set to tour in 1964, the Burke family embarked from the Chevrolet dealership in Providence, Rhode Island. The children dressed alike—the girls in dresses, capes and pillbox hats, the boys in blazers and slacks.

Touring as America's von Trapps

The singing Burke family enjoyed a decade of fame.

W hen my mother was in grammar school, her teacher asked the class what they would like to do when they grew up. My mother was quick to answer: "Well, I'd like to have 10 children—five girls and five boys—and I'd like to travel."

Her teacher, Sister Clare, said, "Anne, dear, those two things don't go together." But somehow my mother found a way to make her special dream come true.

I'm the fifth girl, and my brother Pete the fifth boy, in an Irish Catholic family of 12. My other siblings are Gemma, Anne-Marie, Steve, Walter Jr., Jim, John, Martha and Florrie. We grew up in Peace Dale and then Providence, Rhode Island. My dad, Walter, was an organist and choirmaster who came from a very musical family. Still it was a surprise that all of us children could sing.

Beginning in the early 1960s, our parents packed us up and we traveled together as The Burke Family Singers. We did seven tours,

crisscrossing the United States and Canada in two monogrammed Chevrolet station wagons. We appeared on *The Ed Sullivan Show*, *The Jack Parr Tonight Show* and other television programs.

The press dubbed us the American Trapp Family. We sang with Maria von Trapp and two of her children at a lodge in Stowe, Vermont, in a CBS-TV network special called *The Sound of Christmas*.

Growing up in the tumultuous '60s also gave us a front-row seat to some of the decade's drama. We sang in Montgomery, Alabama, in 1965, the day after the march there from Selma, and tension was thick.

We were a large family from Rhode Island with precious little money. Who would have imagined that we could have had such marvelous experiences while fulfilling the childhood dream my mother expressed to her teacher back in the 1920s?

SARAH JO BURKE · WOODSTOCK, CT

On *The Ed Sullivan Show* at New York City's CBS Studios, Dec. 22, 1963, Walter Burke conducts his family: Florrie, Martha, Anne-Marie, Gemma, Jim, Anne, John and Steve with Walter Jr., Peter and Sarah Jo in front.

THE SOUND OF MUSIC: 20TH CENTURY FOX/KOBAL/SHUTTERSTOCK,
THE WIZARD OF OZ: GEORGE HOMMEL/MGM/KOBAL/SHUTTERSTOCK

In this scene from *The Sound of Music*, Julie Andrews as governess and the actors who portray the von Trapp children sing "The Lonely Goatherd" with its chorus of yodels. The film premiered in 1965 and won five Oscars.

A still from the 1939 movie classic *The Wizard of Oz* shows Judy Garland as Dorothy watching in horror as Bert Lahr's Cowardly Lion bullies Ray Bolger's Scarecrow and Jack Haley's Tin Man. The beloved children's film made its TV debut in 1956.

In their very first collaboration, Richard Rodgers and Oscar Hammerstein penned the breakthrough musical *Oklahoma!* Inspired choreography by Agnes de Mille gave showgoers another reason to love it.

During filming of *Citizen Kane* (1941), star Orson Welles, far right, directed from a wheelchair as he nursed a broken ankle. Dorothy Comingore, far left, played Kane's wife. Cinematographer Gregg Toland, center, adjusts the camera.

'If I Run Into Him'

A green spectator catches Arnold Palmer in a rough spot.

D ateline: Atlanta Athletic Club, 1976. It was the U.S. Open Golf Championship and I had scored two tickets to Wednesday's play; at the time, I worked for a large oil company that was one of the sponsors of the five-day event. As a golf enthusiast, I was thrilled.

Mom agreed to baby-sit our two children while my wife, Jackie, and I joined the spectators. Mom loved to watch golf on television on Sundays, so she asked me, "If possible, would you get Arnold Palmer's autograph?"

"If I run into him," I told her, though the chances were slim.

Once on the course, we found ourselves in the gallery among a throng of spectators. I don't remember which hole it was, but we got to see Palmer's tee shot. With a slight fade to the right, the ball went down the fairway edge and rolled into the rough. The crowd formed a path for Palmer to take a swing out of the rough onto the fairway. Fans stood shoulder to shoulder on each side of the path with a single opening that a person could walk through.

Somewhat bored and hoping to beat the crowd to the next tee, Jackie started looking at the course map to figure out the best route. She was walking as she read, so she wasn't watching where she was going.

Meanwhile, I had stopped to take a look at Palmer hitting out of the rough onto the fairway. When I looked up, I could anticipate what was going to happen next. As if operating in slow motion, Jackie, never raising her head, walked right through the only opening between the bystanders and bumped into Palmer as he entered the fairway.

Of course, she sincerely apologized, while Palmer looked at her as if she was crazy.

Golf legend Arnold Palmer was a showman on the tour.

I started laughing aloud. "Do you know who that was?" I asked her.

"No, who?"

"Arnold Palmer!" Jackie looked unimpressed.

I had told my mom I'd get Palmer's autograph if I ran into him but, as it turned out, my wife was the one who had the collision.

RON METZGER · ROCKWALL, TX

Lookin' Good!

As a spectator during a 1955 golf tournament, my uncle John Court photographed this dapper group of golfers, including Hall of Famer Marvin "Bud" Ward teeing off on a par 5 hole.

CARL VINCENT · MEDICAL LAKE, WA

CHAPTER 9

....

HOLIDAYS AND CELEBRATIONS

When it comes to special occasions,
happiness seems to increase when we
gather with those we love.

Who's Hungry?

Helen, 13, and I couldn't wait to eat our mom's holiday dinner back in 1957. I was 9 when we posed for this photo at the family home in DeWitt, New York. Don't worry, I didn't carve the turkey—Dad handled that duty.

JOHN HAFER · WOODBURY, MN

A Halloween to Remember

Humiliation takes a back seat to winning a costume contest.

When my girlfriend Lynne informed me that we were going to the Halloween night costume ball at the YMCA, I agreed. It was October 1966; I was a senior in high school and happy to have a date. She said her mother was making the costumes, and we were going as Peter Pan and Tinkerbell. Peter would have a really cool outfit, and Tink would wear a pink T-shirt, pink tights and a sequined tutu. She assured me we were going to make a cute couple.

On Halloween, I went over to Lynne's to get dressed for the ball. You can imagine my surprise when I learned the little secret she had kept from me all month—I was the one going as Tinkerbell.

To say I protested would be an understatement. But she batted her baby browns at me and, of course, I gave in. It took months to live down the humiliation and teasing from my guy friends, but I eventually got over it.

We had an enjoyable time at the ball and even ended up winning the grand prize in the costume contest—no money, but it was a happy memory.

Oh, and by the way, the following year Lynne dumped me for a bigger Tinkerbell, the captain of the varsity basketball team. We stayed friends, though, and kept in touch.

JIM MORROW • TUCSON, AZ

On Halloween evening, Deborah, at right, dressed for the party as a flower, while siblings Tom and Phil were clowns, Pete a soldier, Barb Red Riding Hood, Bill an Indian chief, and Gretchen a singer.

DRESSING UP FOR THE MAIN EVENT

GROWING UP, MY SIBLINGS AND I

lived on a farm in Kansas and attended a one-room school. Every year for Halloween, my mother made costumes for me and my six brothers and sisters. Houses in the country were too far apart for trick-or-treating, so we dressed up and went to Mackey Elementary School for a grand annual Halloween party. One time our teacher even wore a bushel basket with long streamers around the edges over her head. We had a parade, bobbed for apples and played games, and the evening ended with apple cider and cookies for everyone.

DEBORAH PACK · NEWPORT NEWS, VA

FALL FEAST
Long after Colonial settlers feasted on fowl, venison and corn, editor Sarah J. Hale petitioned multiple presidents until Abraham Lincoln signed a proclamation on Oct. 3, 1863, making Thanksgiving a national holiday that year.

EASTER SUNDAY

⌄ DRESS REHEARSAL

In 1962, our minister asked us to pose for an Easter picture for the *Herald-Whig* in Quincy, Illinois. So Norbert and I and our children Paul, Mark and Diane went to church at midweek wearing our Sunday best. The kids were confused by it all.
SANDY FRANKENBACH · PALMYRA, MO

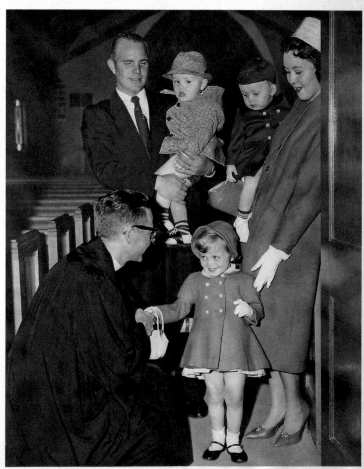

⌃ PLEASE HELP!

I love this photo. In spring 1958, at 14 months old, I was sitting on the lap of a giant, scary-looking Easter Bunny. My sister, Carol, 3½, is smiling, apparently enjoying my distress.
JANE CHRISTIE GIBSON
ALLENTOWN, PA

« BONNY TOTS

Here I am standing with my brother Dean by the picket fence at our family's home in Chillicothe, Ohio, on Easter 1953.
CATHY CARROLL MERCER
BEAVERCREEK, OH

My brother Thomas,
sister Cynthia and I are going
Easter egg hunting in 1962.
Our mom made those dresses.

SUSAN KREISS
ROSEBURG, OR

⌃ CHILDHOOD NOSTALGIA

Many things in addition to our new clothes made Easter special in the early 1960s. Shirley, Richard and Raymond (above) and I (top photo, foreground) would rush home after services at St. Mark AME to hunt for eggs, then we'd visit with Grandma and Grandpop downstairs. Grandma always complimented me for remembering to bring her a palm branch on Palm Sunday. After a little TV watching in the afternoon, we'd sit down to a big meal featuring some of Mom's best cooking of the year.

VINCENT JAMES · ELMONT, NY

« SPRING SMILES

With our new hats, we're ready for the Easter parade! This was in Morristown, Tennessee, in 1941, when I was 7. I'm with my sisters Bonnie, 10, and Peggy, 12, and our brother Billy, 5.

ALICE SHEETS
CENTRAL CITY, NE

Egg seekers rush for the pines during a frantic Easter Sunday event in Alabama in the 1960s.

Egg Hunt Turns Raw

Big prizes send an Easter crowd into a frenzy.

Our family-owned radio stations had been sponsoring small Easter egg hunts for kids for several years. In the early 1960s, we bought a TV station in Huntsville—WAAY-TV, a companion to our radio station—and decided to have a gigantic hunt, with prize slips hidden inside plastic eggs. Most were for discounts on products, but a few were for TVs, and one was for a car.

I had been out of college for only 10 months when I started working at the TV station, but I understood promotion and how to attract large crowds for events. We talked up the egg hunt and its promise of big prizes on both TV and radio for several weeks.

In previous years we were lucky to get a few hundred people searching for about 500 plastic eggs on one of our Easter Sunday events. But

We had only one small megaphone,
which wasn't loud enough to reach
the whole throng at once.

The swelling crowd included kids who were knocked down when the hunt got underway.

for the hunt of 1964, we bought 2,000 plastic eggs, and staffers worked overtime stuffing prize tickets into every one. We scattered the eggs in a pine grove next to the parking lot behind the high school stadium.

I got to the grove about two hours before the 2 p.m. start time on Easter Sunday, our colorful plastic eggs clearly visible among the fallen pine needles.

All too soon, the crowd began to grow by the hundreds, a mix of adults and children, some still in their Easter outfits. We were pleased by the turnout, if a little fearful of it, too. It was far larger than anything we'd handled in the past, and it became clear that we weren't prepared for such numbers. We had only one small megaphone, which wasn't loud enough to reach the whole throng at once. So announcers took turns with it, walking through the parking lot to warn people to stay on the tarmac until the hunt began.

As the clock neared 2 p.m., someone at one end must have yelled something that sounded like "go."

The horde bolted for the grove like cattle running from gunshots. Small kids and their Easter baskets were knocked to the ground as adults descended on the eggs, scooping them into sacks, pillowcases, purses, pockets—whatever they had. The children were lucky not to get trampled, let alone grab an egg. Most of them emerged empty-handed.

It was the scariest thing I'd ever seen—and we'd caused it all.

There were some unhappy parents that day, but thankfully, no one sued us. And our sponsors were pleased with the store traffic generated by the hunt.

Even so, we learned a lot about crowd control that Easter. The next year, we procured a monster 800-watt PA system to communicate with the crowd, and we roped off areas clearly separating the children's hunt from the adult hunt. We ran many more successful giant Easter egg hunts after that, some with as many as 10,000 plastic eggs, and never had a repeat of the Scare of '64.

M.D. SMITH IV · HUNTSVILLE, AL

Postmark North Pole

The annual letter to Santa stoked childhood anticipation and sent mountains of mail to the post office.

Dear Santa,
how are you?

For Christmas I would [like]
the Bratz motorcycle, please!

Katie Weitman

P.S. I can smell Mrs. Claus's
cookies from San Antonio, TX.
and one last thing if you could
mabye get Richard +
I together. I like that, but
please don't tell my mom!

Sam's wishs

Dear Santa,

I hope you have good flying
conditions coming down. I have
been a very good boy. For
Christmas I would like to
have some kind of way to
get a superpowers and take
the power away or back. But
if you can not just give me
a game boy advance or the
bike in the toys'r'us magizine,
which ever one you would think
I would like the most.

Sincerely,
Sam Weitman
P.S. I'm serious about the super
powers.

RETURN TO SENDER
Each year, our children wrote letters to Santa and I would mail
them to their grandma, who would return them to me when
she came to our house for Christmas. This worked well until
the kids wanted to address their own letters. Then I had to
ask our postman to retrieve the letters for me.
JODY WEITMAN · FISH CREEK, WI

⌃ CLASSIC TREE

Taken in 1957, this photo shows me and my big sister, Linda, 8. On her first Christmas, Linda received the 1949 Lionel train set displayed under our Charlie Brown Christmas tree.

BARBARA EUBANKS
ANDERSON, IN

SHORTLISTED FOR 1959 »

Looking back I can't help but laugh at how humble I'd been to ask for only three gifts on the final year Santa would ever bring presents to me.

DEBBIE McNAUGHTON
SOUTH YARMOUTH, MA

Dear Santa??

As you know I am 10 years old this is my last year with you. I do not have much to ask for.

1. United States Games.
2. Junior Typewriter.
3. Jill Doll clothes

P.S. Please get mom a stool

Love Debby Freeman

Merry Merry Christmas
XOXO

Dear Santa,

I would like some slippers that are Eeyore,
I gave you oreos and milk your reindeer get
sparkle food and 1 carrot.

On your letter you wrote that I might get
a CD player I would love that. I would want
some CD's with that, if you could. I would like
Shilo 2, I know I spelt that wrong. Oh well.
I hope you have a great night.

Say hi to Dasher, Dancer, Prancer, Vixen,
Comet, Cupid, Donder, Blizten, and Rudolph.

Also hi to you Santa, and Mrs. Claus and
the elves.

A kid,
Colleen Lynch

P.S. Circle is it Donder or Doner

« KEEPING IT CHATTY
I came across this letter while cleaning out my bedroom bureau drawers. It was written by my youngest daughter, Colleen, when she was 9.
PATTY LYNCH
CHARLESTOWN, MA

Since 1912, the U.S. Postal Service Operation Santa program has spread a little magic by arranging the adoption of letters from children in need, resulting in written responses or the granting of their wishes.

HEADS UP FROM THE HEAD ELF
Back when our daughter, Lisa, was 16, she was a normal hard-to-live-with teenager. That year, I warned her and she got a lump of coal for Christmas. The next year, I got it back. The following year, she received it again. This tit for tat has been going on now for 36 years.
FRANK KOLENDA · GRAND RAPIDS, MI

My Letter To Santa Clause   1960 !

Dear Mr. Clause,

    I have tried to be a good girl throughout the year.I hope
what I ask from you is not too much.Well,I want a watch,
a necklace and bracelet,plastic or glass dishes,doll clothes,
records and a record rack.Thak you for all your time to read my
letter.Please give your signature below.

                        Santa Clause

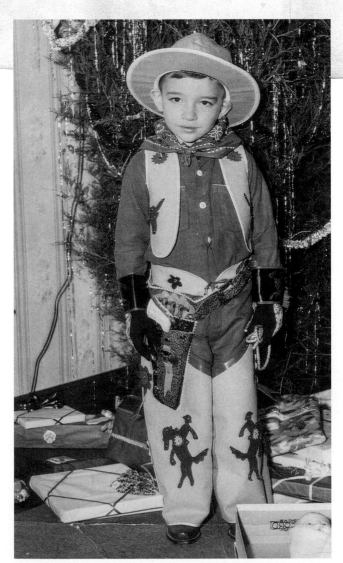

⌃ PROOF OF SIGNATURE

I was 10 in 1960 when I typed this brief letter to Santa. We lived in the country and I remember Daddy making a quick run to the neighborhood store on Christmas Eve, apparently to have a friend sign the letter. My parents were smart enough to know I'd recognize their handwriting.
SHARON PEDIGO · RINGGOLD, GA

« STICK 'EM UP

On Christmas Day 1955 in Danville, Virginia, my son Michael got his wish. Here, he's dressed head to toe in a cowboy outfit complete with holster, gloves and chaps. He always played one of the good guys, making the neighborhood safer for law-abiding folks.
GALE BOULWARE · ARAPAHOE, NC

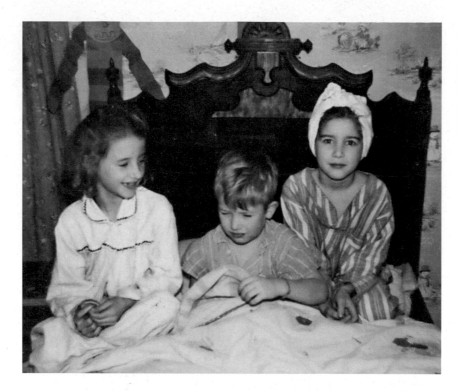

It Takes Planning To Tiptoe Down in Silence

On the biggest day of the year, practice makes perfect.

We had a wonderful childhood growing up in Lockport, New York. One of the highlights of the year was, of course, Christmas.

The stairs to the living room were right outside our parents' bedroom door. If we were going to be successful in sneaking down early to peek at the gifts Santa Claus had left us without waking our parents, we had to know exactly where to place our feet. My sister Susan and I would spend weeks practicing going down the staircase so we could locate the squeaky areas on all of the steps.

By the time the big day came, we were ready. We always managed to sneak downstairs without a hitch—although we never knew for certain whether our parents had heard us. If they had, they never said so.

On Christmas Eve in 1946, our parents came into our bedroom to take our picture. Seven-year-old Susan is smiling at our brother Rob, 4, while I look straight at the camera. I was 6 at the time and my mother had carefully wrapped my hair before bed to keep my bobby-pinned curls in place.

Susan and I were wide awake with anticipation but Rob had been sound asleep.

After the photo, Susan and I went back to our bunk beds on the other side of the room and, although filled with excitement, we fell asleep.

On Christmas morning, we followed through with our well-practiced plan, avoiding all the noisy areas as we tiptoed down the stairs to see the presents under the tree and our stockings full of treasures. Oh, did we have fun!

GAIL THOMAS · VICTOR, NY

The stairs to the living room were right outside our parents' bedroom door.

Like any self-respecting third grader on Christmas Eve, Steve peeked under the tree.

FRIEND ON WHEELS

ANTICIPATION WOKE ME THAT Christmas Eve of 1963. The house was quiet and, aside from the night light in my bedroom, quite dark.

Naturally, I did what any other 8-year-old would do under similar circumstances: I went to sneak a peek at the array of presents under the Christmas tree.

Even in the unlit room I could see all the wrapped gifts, and an unwrapped one that immediately drew my full attention: a bicycle!

Going in for a closer look, I saw a gift tag on the bike but I couldn't quite make it out, so I carefully removed it and took it back to my bedroom for inspection.

There, under the soft glow of my trusty night light, the words leapt right off the tag: "To Steve from Santa."

I was beside myself with joy!

I very carefully reattached the gift tag to the fender and caressed the bike's leather-textured seat a couple of times before going back to bed, basking in the knowledge that Santa had brought me my most perfect present.

Of course, after that I couldn't sleep. Desperate for daylight to come, I gathered my pillow and blanket and camped out on the hard oak floor just outside my bedroom door—from there, it was a mere three steps down the stairs and then a few more across the living room to where my bicycle was waiting for me.

Later that morning, when the rest of my family finally got up, I learned that my new bicycle was a Hercules three-speed with motorcycle-style handlebar shifting and real hand brakes.

Despite the cold and, later that afternoon, the snow, the Hercules and I became better acquainted as we toured the neighborhood.

The bicycle and I remained faithful friends for years—that is, until the day I got my driver's license. Only then did my mom's Malibu station wagon become my new bestest buddy.

STEPHEN RUSINIAK · WAYNE, NJ

TIME TO PLAY
My cousin Hector "Papo" Duran plays with his new toys in a treasured family photo taken at Hector's home in New York. The toy service station behind him even has a soda fountain.
NORMA PETTIT
PLACERVILLE, CA

HOLIDAY GIFTING

Presents for the lady of the house certainly allow for a bit of beauty.

Natural Inspiration

In a *Better Homes and Gardens* magazine ad, these jewelry selections from Krementz bring a touch of the natural world with likenesses of flowers, holly and evergreen branches to decorate the wearer.

Love at First Sight

The young woman illustrated in this ad couldn't be happier to receive a complete service for eight of Community silverware. Romance is cleverly intermingled with the optional set designs and the couple under the mistletoe.

THANK YOU SANTA

⌄ JUST RIGHT FOR TEA

For Christmas 1959, my dad, Harry Borgfield, made this modern-looking table and chair set for me, left, and my older sister Karen in the hobby shop on the Spangdahlem Air Base in Germany where he was stationed.

CHERYL HARDT · HIGH RIDGE, MO

FUELING
A PASSION »

Ever since he was young, my son Tim has loved the idea of being a farmer. Here he is, 4, in 1968, showing off the John Deere toy tractor set he got for Christmas. Today, he collects full-grown tractors, but he still has that toy collection. And after all these years, he's kept it in pretty good shape.

DAVID NICHOLAS
LAWRENCE, MI

⌃ WALK LIKE A ROBOT

On Christmas Day in 1945, Santa delivered a big red metal box containing the largest Erector Set on the market. It had two electric motors and metal parts to build an almost infinite assortment of devices, including a robot. That idea fascinated me, so I immediately got to work. What resulted was a wonderful 2-foot-tall metal man with lightbulb eyes and motorized legs capable of walking. I brought my robot to school and showed him to the class.

Within days I received a telephone call from KSL Radio inviting me for a live interview on one of their programs. I gladly accepted, arriving on Saturday morning for the interview. They even took a picture.

FRANKLIN L. CHILD · HOLLADAY, UT

THANK YOU SANTA

« GLOWING GIRLS

My sister Diane, right, holds her Tiny Tears doll and I'm wearing my new Timex watch. We'd celebrate with family on Christmas Eve and get home to find Santa had come. As we waited in the car to go to Grandma's, we never understood why it took our mother so long to come out of the house.
CECILIA FRANCIS · BALLWIN, MO

READY TO RIDE »

My brother Bryan and I woke up that holiday at home in Beaumont to find unexpected toys under the tree—a bike for him and a pedal tractor for me. I learned to ride Bryan's bike the next year.
DOYLE WELBORN · KOUNTZE, TX

CHRISTMAS SPOILS »
It looks as if we all got what we asked for that year, judging by the smiles on our faces. At the Lyons family home in Monaca are my sister Judy and I with our brothers Tim, David and Paul.
SUSAN LYONS DIETRICH
MONACA, PA

⌃ ROBED FOR ADVENTURE
My brothers Joe and Jeff wield six-shooters, and I'm armed with a jet and a car to round out the unbeatable Groom posse at the family home in Columbus.
GREG GROOM · COLUMBUS, OH

Holiday Surprises

A roadside run-in and a barnyard swap
made for an unforgettable Christmas.

Christmas Eve 1952 in rural Alabama held quite the adventure for our family, followed by a gift the next day that was completely unexpected.

My dad, Luther McPherson, was the pastor of a small church in Surry County, North Carolina, a two-hour drive from where we lived. The houses were scattered, so no one had any close neighbors.

As was the custom in those days in many southern churches, members of the congregation gave my dad and our family what was called a pounding—gifts of nonperishable food items to stock our pantry.

On our way home that night, the car died. Dad went for help, leaving my mother, Martha, with me and my brother David in the wilderness.

A short time later, lights appeared; men armed with rifles surrounded us and shined flashlights in every window. They asked questions about all the presents and food in the car. Mother was terrified. My brother and I welcomed the excitement.

The posse, it seems, was searching for someone who had broken into nearby houses and stolen food and gifts. One man, a member of our church, recognized my mother, and explained to the group why our car was loaded with gifts.

My dad soon returned with help, got the engine started, and we drove home, where another surprise awaited David and me.

Christmas morning, my brother and I woke early to find a saddle under our tree. We were confused, but Dad told us to look in the barn.

Sure enough, there we found a pony and a cart.

By this time, it was getting light and time to feed the chickens, milk the goat and slop the three pigs. That's when we realized two pigs were missing. It seems Santa had swapped the pigs for a pony, who we named Dolly.

We never figured out how Santa had managed it, but that was our best Christmas ever.

PAT McPHERSON · MOUNT GILEAD, NC

My dad soon returned with help, got the engine started, and we drove home, where another surprise awaited David and me.

Little Helper

Holding a box nearly as big as me, I helped this man—not knowing
he was creating a display for Christmas Seals—at the post office in
Modesto in 1966. The photo was used in a fundraising campaign.

LISA MERRILL · SAN DIEGO, CA

CHAPTER 10

LAST LAUGH

Have a good chuckle with these funny
stories of mishaps, miscommunications
and plain ol' silly circumstances.

It's a Long Story About the Shorts

While a student at Nathan Hale High School in West Allis, Wisconsin, in 1944, I delivered sacks of feed and flour three times a week for 25 cents an hour. My mother used one of the flower-print sacks to make me a pair of track shorts. She even sewed a ruffle on the cuffs and added a tiny bell to each side seam. I made music with every jump of the hurdle. I graduated shortly after this photo was taken and joined the Army—but I left those shorts at home.

DIRK VAN DUZEE · WABENO, WI

Arlo became a teacher at 19 (top) and kept smiling throughout his two years at a one-room school. At left, with his students, he is at his desk in front of the bookcase.

NEVER TOO BUSY TO SMILE

MY FIRST YEAR AS A TEACHER, 1948, I was 19 years old and taught 19 children spanning six grades in a one-room schoolhouse near Shawano, Wisconsin. Most of the students were related to each other; in one case, a boy in fourth grade was the uncle of a second grader.

Looking back, I think I did a few key things right. I treated the children like they were my younger brothers and sisters. I taught them to sing, which we did together every day. And I appreciated humor, though what was funny to me was not always funny to the children.

Once, when I saw a boy push a girl while she was getting a drink of water, I told him to go to the end of the line. After a few moments, he came back, whimpering, "There's already somebody there."

"Where?" I asked.

"At the end of the line!"

And there was the time two fourth grade girls came in and one said, "My sister Grace in high school has periods now."

I was suddenly nervous, wondering what I would say if the girls decided to explore the topic or ask my advice. Then the fourth grader added, "She likes the last one in the afternoon the best. That's when she has music."

I wiped my brow in relief.

ARLO JANSSEN · BENSON, AZ

My first school lunch must've been good, because I sat on the porch to finish it long after lunch period ended.

MARVIN MEYER · REDLANDS, CA

The Great Celery Flood of 1971

An inventive rebellion against the clean-your-plate club.

C elery is dull. It has none of the appeal of its showier cousin the carrot. More important, to the third grade mind, celery lacks the projectile power of the pea or the concussion-producing potential of the bulky Brussels sprout. Worse, uneaten celery is almost impossible to hide in a lunchroom with a rigid adherence to the clean-your-plate principle.

It was Miss Brewster's job to verify that we'd cleaned our plates. Tall and thin in her pencil skirt, and topped with a bouffant so blond that it was almost white, Miss Brewster resembled a 6-foot Q-tip stalking the aisles of our school lunchroom. She required proof that we'd eaten the last crumb of our lunch before she'd let us go out for recess.

We tried many methods to dispose of the hated vegetable. One solution was to give it to someone else. The Johnson kid tolerated celery well enough, but not on the scale needed to serve the disposal needs of the entire third grade. My best friend, Dan, invented the milk carton ruse, which met with success for a time—until our friend Rick got sloppy and allowed a couple of green tendrils to protrude from his carton. Brewster made all of us open our milk cartons, exposing the contraband. No recess that day.

Then, desperation to get to the monkey bars led me to stuff the celery into my sock. I presented my clean tray to Miss Brewster—and it worked, though we still had the dilemma of what to do with the smuggled celery once outside the lunchroom. Dumping it on the playground wasn't an option; the authorities would hardly miss a heap of moldering celery in the four-square court.

Then we hit on the boys bathroom, that haven far from Miss Brewster's vigilant eye. Soon every boy was making a pit stop to flush his day's dose of stringy vegetable.

Unfortunately we soon realized the downside of what had seemed our perfect crime. The principal announced that the boys restroom would be out of order due to some unusual plumbing problems. Peeking out of the classroom door, we were horrified to see water flooding the entire hallway and janitors frantically mopping the ever-expanding flow.

None of us said a thing, but from then on, we ate every inch of our lunchtime celery ration.

DOUGLAS WERMEDAL · VOLGA, SD

Doug later found romance with his wife, Deborah, at a Bible college in Cedar Springs.

A Notable Mistake

He learned he had to be himself, especially in love letters.

During the summer of 1966, I was 16 and often rode my bike to the Wednesday night youth meetings at the Free Methodist Church on Main Street. Many of my friends also went because the young pastor enjoyed being around teens and working with them.

One night I expected the usual crowd, but was distracted by a beautiful blond, blue-eyed girl sitting across the aisle several pews back. I asked one of my friends who she was. Tom told me she was Lorraine's cousin. Lorraine was Tom's girlfriend and they had been dating for two years.

If I were to confide in anyone about dating girls, Tom would be the one. Tom was a good friend and I knew I could count on his help.

His first piece of advice was that I write a letter to the young lady telling her about myself and include a picture. Then he added, "That's all you need. I'll help you write some good stuff."

Good stuff? The letter he wrote was filled with more X's and O's than an entire year of *The Dating Game*. All I had to do was sign my name, address the envelope, put on a stamp and send it. I couldn't wait for her reply.

After two weeks, I started to doubt the girl would ever write back. But eventually I went to the mailbox and found a letter addressed to me. *This was going to be the best day of my life.*

I took the envelope to my room so my mother wouldn't get suspicious. I carefully opened it and pulled out a picture. *Great*, I thought, *she sent me hers*. Not so fast—it was the picture I had sent her.

As it turned out, the letter was addressed to me, but was written by the girl's mother—an entire page telling me that her daughter was much too young to get into a serious relationship with someone she had never met. She was courteous, but straightforward.

The more I read, the more embarrassed and ridiculous I felt. So much for my friend Tom and his help. Never again did I trust someone else's advice in making a love connection. I stuck with reading comic books.

DOUGLAS MAXSON · CEDAR SPRINGS, MI

Cricket Chirp Became a Bad Earworm

It was a solo performance they couldn't tune out.

On the day my father left for a five-day conference, I rushed home from school to tell Mom that I was finally understanding long division. But she had something else on her mind.

"A cricket must've hopped inside the piano," she said. "It's been driving me crazy."

I helped her lift the top of our antique Steinway grand, but we couldn't see the insect. Mom called the pet store to see if there was such a thing as a cricket trap. There wasn't, but the manager suggested luring ours with a bit of carrot or potato. We went to bed that night hoping to find the intruder eating its breakfast the next day. In the morning, I did encounter the cricket—chirping inside the piano.

That afternoon, several neighbors stopped by to hear the one-note serenade. One put a stick in the Steinway, thinking the cricket could use it to crawl out. I kept watch, but the cricket was a no-show.

Over the next few days, Mom retreated to the bedroom or bathroom to escape that relentless chirping, and practically every neighbor on the street came by with different kinds of food to attract the insect. The poor piano was groaning under the weight.

When Dad finally came home at the end of the week, he took one look at us and asked, "Is something wrong?"

So we related the Saga of the Cricket. As we spoke, my father leaned over the piano, at which point the stowaway, as if on cue, let out a peep.

Then Dad did something unexpected. He reached behind the Steinway and grabbed the smoke alarm on the wall. The thing chirped in what sounded like delight, while Mom and I stared in complete disbelief.

"It sounds like a cricket when it needs a new battery," Dad said.

Mom collapsed on the couch with a moan. "Wait until the neighbors hear about this."

NANCY O'CONNOR · CARPINTERIA, CA

Feeling the Heat

The brass had a chilly reaction
to his warm-hearted gesture.

Near the end of the Korean War, I was a young Marine officer serving in the Outpost line. Winter, with its 25-below-zero nights, was coming on, and our battalion chaplain thought we could help some of the people in the local village by asking friends and family back home for donations of warm clothing.

A gung-ho second lieutenant named Dudley Floren wrote to his parents, passing along the chaplain's request. As an afterthought, Dudley suggested they send everything collect, and he would pay the postage.

Next, Dudley, who did nothing in a small way, took the project a giant leap further: He wrote to his brother Myron Floren, the star accordion player who regularly performed on *The Lawrence Welk Show*, to appeal for donations during his next TV appearance. And Dudley reminded his brother to say that all postage would be paid.

Sure enough, packages of winter clothing began to pile up at the battalion postal tent and soon overwhelmed the clerk, who shut down the office. No one in the battalion was getting mail. It got worse. The division's post office was inundated, too, and promptly shut down, which meant no one in the entire First Marines could get any mail.

Dudley had to answer first to the battalion commander, then the regiment commander, and finally the commanding general. Desperate, he wrote Myron again, urging him to tell TV viewers to stop the donations, but it could take a month for a letter to reach home. Meanwhile, the clothes kept coming and Dudley's postal bill kept climbing. It hit $24,000—at a time when a second lieutenant's base pay was $222 a month.

I'll never forget the sight of that hill of unwanted coats outside the command post covered with snow, which had started to fall.

TOM C. McKENNEY · OCEAN SPRINGS, MS

ILLUSTRATION: TIM BOWER

Trevose Fire Company volunteers pose after putting out a blaze in 1969. Wayne is third from the left.

The Ford and the Firecrackers

Prankster learns a lesson in an explosive way.

The guys from Trevose Fire Company in Pennsylvania were headed home from a fire and rescue competition when we stopped off at a fireworks shop called South of the Border to stock up on cherry bombs, strings of twenty 2-inchers, bottle rockets—the works.

Known as pranksters, we spent the next few months finding ways to use the fireworks to surprise the older guys in the firehouse. They never saw the humor in our fun and were glad when our supply began to dwindle.

But one fall day, with my last stash of 2-inchers beside me on the front seat of my 1956 Ford Fairlane Victoria, I drove to the firehouse. My car, only 3 years old, was in mint condition and super quiet, so no one turned around when I drove up. Pushing in my cigarette lighter, I lit the fuse on a firecracker and tossed it out my window, and it landed directly behind my best friend.

When I heard a hissing sound, I realized that the lit fuse had come off and landed in the middle of the remaining string of 2-inchers on my front seat. I quickly jumped out of my car and slammed the door shut.

Meanwhile, all my buddies turned around in time to see the string of firecrackers exploding inside my beloved automobile.

At first, they were shocked as they watched my car fill with blue smoke. Then they noticed the unexploded firecracker at their feet and knew what had happened.

When the laughter and smoke subsided, I walked to the car to assess the damage. On the upside, my car didn't catch fire. That would have been the ultimate embarrassment—a firefighter burning up his own vehicle. Still, the entire interior had to be replaced due to smoke damage.

With my firehouse friends still smiling, I shook my head and made a mental note never to play a practical joke again. Or at least not one that involved firecrackers.

WAYNE MOYER · MIDLOTHIAN, VA

Nuns, Snakes and Bad Polaroids

Travels with Dad were always a trip.

When I was 13, my parents decided to take my 9-year-old brother, Barry, and me on a trip to Canada. Before we left Massachusetts, we stopped for a fill-up. The station owner—a friend of Dad's—suggested we stay at a place he knew just over the border. "It's run by some nuns," he added.

This was 1960, so navigation was done via giant folding map. In Quebec, we bumped along back roads until we came to an edifice the size of a medieval abbey. Once inside, a nun brought us a large tureen of soup.

"Sister," my mother said, "it was our understanding this is a hotel." The nun shook her head. In broken English, she managed to convey that the place was, in fact, a homeless shelter. Horrified, Mom glared at Dad.

The nuns arranged for us to stay with a farm family nearby. A boy showed Mom and me to

a bed fitted with round jar caps filled with liquid. "They are just to keep the snakes out," he reassured us. We clambered onto the bed and didn't touch the floor the rest of the night.

The next morning, we heard Dad snapping Polaroids of our hosts. His pictures were always terrible, with vital body parts cut off, but the family didn't mind.

The rest of our trip was just as eventful. In Quebec City, Dad tried to take our photo at the Citadel, the fortress above the St. Lawrence River, but he backed up too far and went over the wall.

"What should we do?" I asked my mother.

"Pretend you don't know him," she replied.

In Montreal, he lost his wallet and we had to call my aunt to wire us money. Then Dad realized he'd lost our suitcases.

More mishaps—including Dad and Barry sinking their rented paddleboat—didn't break our spirits. As we made our way home, Dad asked, "How about going to Washington next year?"

Unfortunately, we did.

MELVA MICHAELIAN
SPRINGFIELD, MA

ILLUSTRATION: TIM BOWER

GO WITH HUMOR

Getting a laugh from a potential customer gets their attention and maybe their business.

1949 »

No Scares Here

It's hard not to smile at the little ghost in the corner of this ad. No chills or "creeps" for you. Hanes promises that its GIVVIES will stretch and stay put.

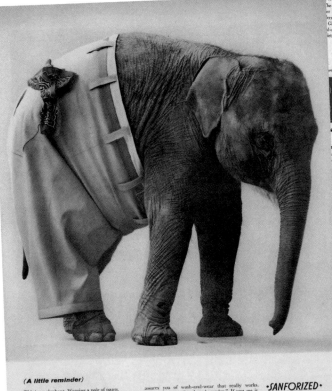

« 1963

Giant Claim

These "Sanforized-Plus" pants promise to be wash-and-wear with this eye-catching ad: "The elephant is wrinkled," it says. "It's not his fault. He was made that way. The pants are never wrinkled. They were made that way, too."

On a Steel Horse He Rides

Those cowboys made it look easy.

Mark's faithful Murray bike took a bad turn the day he tried to imitate TV good guys.

Back in 1957, I was 9 years old and living in Parma, Ohio, though I dreamed of the Old West when I watched my favorite shows such as *The Lone Ranger*, *The Cisco Kid*, *Hopalong Cassidy* and other TV Westerns.

My house was only a few houses away from my elementary school, so I often rode my "horse"—actually, my trusty 20-inch Murray bicycle—to the playground in the summer.

One day as I was riding I came up with a great idea. I remembered how the cowboys would leap off their horses to jump on a bad guy, and thought I should be able to do the same thing. My target wasn't a bad guy, but the park's merry-go-round.

I peddled fast to work up a good head of speed and zoomed toward my goal. Amazingly, I jumped off my bike and leaped onto the ride without even a scratch!

The Murray, however, was not so fortunate. It kept going and careened straight into the playground fence. What made the situation worse was that my dad had just arrived home from work and was standing on the other side of the fence at the moment of impact.

He wasn't impressed when I told him a real horse would've known how to stop.

MARK STEFFEN · WASHBURN, TN

ALL IN THE NAME

FOR YEARS I DELIVERED MEALS ON WHEELS to a lady named Adelaide Healey. She was no relation to me, but we became good friends and shared lots of laughs. At the time I was about 63 and she was close to 90.

Adelaide had to have surgery and was recovering at her home, where a visiting nurse came to see her. I was at her house one day when the nurse came by. When I answered the door, the nurse asked if Mrs. Healey was in. I saw a once-in-a-lifetime opportunity, and I jumped at it.

"Yes, she is," I told the nurse. "And I'm Mr. Healey." Then I called out loudly, "Darling, there's a lady here to see you."

When Adelaide came to the door, the nurse openly stared at her and then at me. She kept looking at us throughout the home visit, obviously puzzled. Adelaide and I were laughing but we never told the woman we weren't married.

JIM HEALEY · APTOS, CA

Don't Look Behind that Door!

Double surprise ends up in arrest.

Our daughter Tina Ann was 12 when we moved into an older home in the Sunnyslope neighborhood of Phoenix. We'd warned her a few times not to slam the back door on the house because there was a crack in the window glass and we didn't want the window to shatter.

One day when I was in the kitchen cutting up a large watermelon with a butcher knife, I heard the back door slam very hard. I hurried to the back room, intending to scold Tina Ann, but she wasn't there. I guessed she must have been going out the door, not in. I was about to call her when I heard a noise in the washer/dryer closet. She knows she's in trouble and she's hiding, I thought. Thinking to surprise her, I tiptoed to the closet, yanked open the door and yelled, "What are you doing in there?"

Except it wasn't Tina Ann. It was a man, a stranger, who pushed past me and escaped out the back door. I dropped the knife and ran to my husband in the front room, yelling about the strange man I'd just seen.

At that point we heard a commotion outside and saw several policemen coming up the street. We told them about our intruder and, after a quick search, the cops found him hiding in a neighbor's yard.

Later we learned that our intruder and another man had been shopping at a nearby bookstore when the clerk saw them stealing and called the police. During the arrest, one of the men had broken away and run off, ending up in our backyard. When he found our door unlocked, he decided to hide inside the house.

I don't know who was more frightened that day, me at finding a stranger in the house or the intruder at being confronted by an angry woman with a butcher knife. The only one who thought it was funny was Tina Ann.

MARY ANN GOVE · PHOENIX, AZ

Essay Got Her Fired

Oops! That wasn't supposed to be published.

As an enthusiastic student in Miss Heeren's journalism class in Denison (Iowa) High School during World War II, I worked hard to develop my storytelling skills. And Miss Heeren encouraged my love of writing. To this day I am grateful for her guidance.

I still have a newspaper clipping, yellowed now, from April 1944: "Paula Runge was awarded first place with an original short story in the Drake University creative writing contest." I had no idea that Miss Heeren had entered my school assignment in a national contest. As a budding writer, I felt pretty good about that award.

Another time, Miss Heeren apparently liked an assigned piece of mine so much that she had it published as a surprise. Unfortunately, this one did not end with me receiving an award. In fact, the result was something of a disaster.

It was a story about my part-time, 33-cents-an-hour job at the department store in our small town. In it I discussed how we high school girls liked to hide in the sewing section to giggle and gossip. Though Mr. Bloom and the other managers diligently monitored the sales floor at all times from their mezzanine offices, they couldn't see us behind the large bolts of fabric.

I also revealed some other secret on-the-job habits we had, such as how we'd linger for a few extra minutes in the restroom for covert cigarette smoking.

Imagine my dismay when my tell-all appeared published in the school paper. Someone—maybe everyone—must have shown Mr. Bloom my purple prose. Denison had a population of about 5,000 back then, so hot news was all over town in less than an hour.

I didn't have to be formally fired; I just knew that I was.

Fortunately, my parents laughed about it, and their only comment was that Mr. Bloom didn't have much of a sense of humor. It also was comforting when my mom said Mrs. McHenry, the city librarian, had told her my essay compared with those in *The New Yorker*.

I don't know if Miss Heeren heard about my job loss, but I never mentioned it to her. Actually, part of me was glad to have Saturdays and Sundays free.

I still think of Miss Heeren when I'm on my computer, but looking back I wonder if my essay should have been titled, Why Teenagers Are Pretty Much Unemployable.

PAULA RUNGE HASSLER · TEMPE, AZ

NO PRIVACY HERE

WE HAD ONE HOME PHONE WHILE growing up in Baldwinsville, New York. It was a black rotary wall phone that hung in a corner of the kitchen for 40 years until Mom sold the house in 1994. I fought with my three brothers and sister for talk time, and since the phone was in the kitchen, privacy was nonexistent. Chatting on the phone, we would doodle and carve into the sill of the window that looked out on the backyard. At first Mom would yell and try to stop us, but she soon gave up and let us have that little space for our creativity. Over the years, the sill became our legacy. Our mom is now gone and we are all over 60 with smartphones. But we still remember that kitchen wall phone and the window sill.

BONNIE FOWLER · FARMINGTON, NY

Sometimes called camera or coffin phones, early wall phones connected to networks by turning the crank.

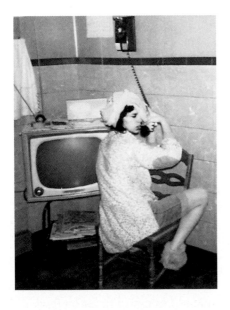

Bonnie at 16 cherished her moments of phone time to tell friends about the cute boy she said hi to that day.

WHICH END IS UP?

OUR 100-YEAR-OLD HOUSE IN BUCKINGHAM County, Virginia, had no electricity, plumbing, central heating or phone. I had seen a telephone—a wooden box on the wall—at a relative's house. After I graduated from high school in 1944, I moved to Richmond where I found a job as a messenger at an Army facility. Within the first hour, personnel called my supervisor, who instructed me to answer the phone. I didn't see a wall box, but she pointed to the black object sitting on her desk. "Right there," she said. A cord led to a handset so I picked it up and said "Hello," but heard nothing. Then the supervisor reached over, turned the handset 180 degrees and said, "You'll hear better like this."

RUPERT FERGUSON · NORTH CHESTERFIELD, VA

In the '60s, my girls would act up and fight whenever I got on the phone. Boy, were they surprised when I got a longer cord and could walk into their rooms.

CAROL LINCE · GAYLORD, MI

A Reel Mess

That was one experience he wished he could rewind.

The Projectionist Club was among the after-school groups offered at E.W. Thurston Junior High School in Westwood when I was in seventh grade. It trained students how to use the school's audiovisual equipment, including reel-to-reel tape recorders, record players and projectors. Once trained, club members would operate the equipment for the teachers during classes.

The training was intense, and you had to pass a written test and do a demonstration. But you received a Bell & Howell qualified projectionist certificate, lapel pin and operator's license.

In my quest for that coveted license, I ended up in an embarrassing jam—and in front of most of the school.

Several social studies classes had gathered in the auditorium to watch a movie. When the teacher called for a member of the Projectionist Club to run the equipment, my classmates volunteered me, even though it was still September and our club had met only a couple of times.

But in those days, you did what a teacher ordered without question. Fortunately, our first two club meetings had covered how to run the auditorium's 16 mm projector, so I felt I could handle it.

As it turned out, I knew just enough to be dangerous. I looped the lead from the reel into the projector and around the sprockets, locked the film in place and turned on the machine. All went well for several minutes until the film began to jump. We'd been told about this, so I knew what to do: I opened the door on the side of the projector to fix the tracking—only to be greeted by a giant tangle of film that spilled onto the floor. In my haste, I hadn't fed the movie onto the takeup reel properly.

Realizing the hopelessness of the situation, the teacher sent everyone back to their classrooms. Meanwhile, there I stood in a pile of film reaching almost to my knees. As people filed out I heard a teacher grumble, "and we were just getting to the best part."

Undaunted, I remained in the club and a few months later became a qualified projectionist.

That club taught me about the importance of hard work and perseverance, which is why I've kept the awards I earned.

By the way, I never again had a problem running the AV equipment at school—or later, when I became a teacher.

FRANK COOK · ATTLEBORO, MA

As it turned out, I knew just enough to be dangerous.

Buyer Could Smell a Bargain

Looking for a deal on a dead mudfish.

Down the street in my old neighborhood in Darlington, South Carolina, was a pond where one day in the summer of 1976, my friend Danny and I decided to try rig fishing. I'd read about the technique in *Field and Stream*: You attach a baited line to an overhanging tree branch, and when the fish hits the line, it sets the hook. We baited the rig line with a smaller fish and bided our time upstream.

Meanwhile Danny's brother David showed up with a couple of his friends. They weren't all that interested in our fishing experiment—that is, until it worked. With a loud *BAM!* the tree limb slapped the water with the weight of a huge fish that was splashing wildly.

We managed to get it onto the bank and saw that it was a mudfish, or bowfin as some call it, as long as my leg.

One of the boys suggested we sell it in town. Some of the old locals love this type of fish, he said, and they know how to clean it. (It's tricky, as mudfish are very bony.) So Danny and I picked up our catch, and the five of us headed into town about a mile away.

We hit a live one at the first place we stopped.

"That's a good fish you got there," the shop owner said. "I'll give you $3 for it." He told us to divide the money five ways.

"But Danny and I were the ones who caught it," I protested. "These other guys were just spectators."

The man was quite firm. "Share or no deal."

Danny and I thought about it and decided it was no deal. We lugged that smelly thing around town, store to store, the rest of the afternoon—and guess what? No one else was interested in a dead mudfish.

So we ended up back at the first shop, where the owner was still willing to take it off our hands, but at a new price. This time, he offered us the grand sum of $1.

Danny and I didn't even have to think about it. It was a deal!

ADAM SIBCY · MAYSVILLE, GA

Costume Race

This image was taken by my Uncle Merle, who started skiing in the 1940s. Merle Belling traveled across country with his Argos camera, capturing fellow skiers in action and having fun, like in this shot.

CHUCK BELLING · MADISON, WI